# Severe and
# Enduring Eating
# Disorder

D1332108

# Severe and Enduring Eating Disorder (SEED)

## Management of Complex Presentations of Anorexia and Bulimia Nervosa

**Paul Robinson**

**WILEY-BLACKWELL**

A John Wiley & Sons, Ltd, Publication

Wiley-Blackwell is an imprint of John Wiley & Sons, formed by the merger of Wiley's global Scientific, Technical, and Medical business with Blackwell Publishing.

*Registered Office*
John Wiley & Sons Ltd, The Atrium, Southern Gate, Chichester, West Sussex, PO19 8SQ, UK

*Editorial Offices*
The Atrium, Southern Gate, Chichester, West Sussex, PO19 8SQ, UK
9600 Garsington Road, Oxford, OX4 2DQ, UK
350 Main Street, Malden, MA 02148-5020, USA

For details of our global editorial offices, for customer services, and for information about how to apply for permission to reuse the copyright material in this book please see our website at www.wiley.com/wiley-blackwell.

**Library of Congress Cataloging-in-Publication Data**

Robinson, Paul H., Dr.
  Severe and enduring eating disorder (SEED) : management of complex presentations of anorexia and bulimia nervosa / Paul Robinson.
    p. ; cm.
  Includes bibliographical references and index.
  ISBN 978-0-470-06206-7 (cloth) – ISBN 978-0-470-06207-4   1. Eating disorders–Treatment. I. Title.
  [DNLM:  1. Anorexia Nervosa.  2. Bulimia Nervosa. WM 175 R663s 2009]
  RC552.E18.R623 2009
  616.85′26206–dc22

                                                                                    2008055189

A catalogue record for this book is available from the British Library.

Set in 10.5/13pt Minion by Aptara Inc., New Delhi, India.
Printed and bound in Singapore by Fabulous Printers Pte Ltd

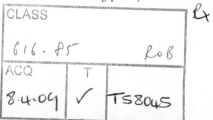

*To the patients, and their families, who granted
me their confidence.*

# Contents

# Clinical Descriptions

**Chapter 1**

Patient A: Chronic and life-threatening, but apparently not "Severe and Enduring".
Patient B: Anorexia Nervosa, auditory hallucinations, somatoform disorder and sexual abuse.
Patient C: Chronically stable low weight, obsessive cleaning, social isolation.
Patient D: Anorexia Nervosa, poor attachments.
Patient E: Consultant, therapist disagreement reflects parental dynamics.

**Chapter 2**

Patient F: Condiment abuse in Anorexia Nervosa
Patient G: Where's that strange smell coming from?
Patient B (continued): PTSD treated with EMDR
Patient H: SEED-AN. Prolonged inpatient treatment, far from home. Severe depression, self harm, attempted suicide.
Patient I: Anorexia Nervosa, epilepsy, somatization, obsessive compulsive disorder and hoarding.
Patient J: Obsessional house cleaning
Patient K: Anorexia and bulimia nervosa, deliberate self-harm, drug and alcohol abuse and mood swings treated by repeated brief private admissions.

**Chapter 3**

Patient L: Anorexia and bulimia nervosa, food allergies and Irritable Bowel Syndrome. A potentially fatal combination.
Patient M: Record waterloading of 10 litres caused fits.

# About the Author

Dr Paul Robinson in a Consultant Psychiatrist in Eating Disorders Psychiatry at the Russell Unit Eating Disorders Service, part of the St Ann's Eating Disorders Service, Barnet Enfield and Haringey Mental Health Trust. After postgraduate training in medicine, psychiatry and family therapy, he conducted research into the physical determinants of food intake in eating disorders at Johns Hopkins Medical School, Baltimore, and the Institute of Psychiatry and now has been working in Eating Disorders Psychiatry for 23 years. His interests over the last 11 years have been in the community care of severely ill patients with eating disorders and the use of e-mail to deliver treatment for eating disorders. He lives in North London with his wife, Sonja Linden, a playwright.

# Preface

## Organization of This Book

Chapter 1 introduces the idea of SEED and its relationship to SEMI (severe and enduring mental illness). In addition, the complementary concepts of 'Handicap and Adaptation', 'Models of Illness' and the domains introduced with Care Programme Approach are covered.

The next part of the book (Chapters 3–5) is arranged such that each major domain has its own chapter. Psychiatric disorders in SEED are described in Chapter 2, according to whether they are attributable to malnutrition, disturbed body image or other origins. Medical monitoring and the assessment and management of chronic medical problems such as osteoporosis are covered in Chapter 3. Social and occupational problems, including those associated with accommodation, food shopping and consumption, finances, occupation, social networking and transport, are described in Chapter 4; issues arising in different family constellations are described in Chapter 5. Family of origin, family of creation and independent living are considered, as are eating disordered children of divorced parents, siblings and the children of eating disordered mothers. In each of these chapters, the problems of SEED are illustrated by reference to specific patients. Their histories have been changed to protect their identity, but the essentials remain. Chapter 6 aims to integrate the assessment process and introduce comprehensive management under the Care Programme Approach, and the results of a pilot study of a group of patients with SEED are presented in Chapter 7. Chapter 8 compares the concept of SEED with the severe and enduring category as applied to schizophrenia, and in Chapter 9 a number of potential research ideas in the field are listed and organized according to the chapter in which the area is described. The book ends with a glossary of terms (some eight neologisms are proposed) and an index.

# Acknowledgements

I am indebted to my colleagues in the emerging sub-specialty of Eating Disorders Psychiatry who have taught me so much, particularly Gerald Russell and the late Arthur Crisp, as well as Janet Treasure, Chris Dare, Ivan Eisler, Ulrike Schmidt and Bob Palmer, who each bring their own unique clinical and investigative approach to this absorbing subject.

Secondly, I am profoundly grateful to the wonderful members of the Russell Unit team who, since I arrived there in 1997, have shown me what can be done by a group of talented, energetic, flexible and imaginative people for individuals with severe and enduring eating disorders.

The references to inpatient treatment allude to experiences at the Capio Nightingale Hospital, to whose excellent staff I am very grateful.

A particular thank you goes to Navsheer Gill, University of East Anglia School of Medicine, who conducted interviews with a number of patients with SEED whose histories appear in the book.

I am grateful to the editorial and production staff of John Wiley & Sons who have done such an excellent job in helping this book and its precursor from computer file to bookshop.

Chapter 7 was co-written with Dr Jamie Arkell who is a Consultant in General Adult Psychiatry at the South Kensington and Chelsea Mental Health Centre, which is part of Central North West London Mental Health Trust. He has postgraduate training in family therapy and cognitive behavioural therapy. He sits on the development board at The Almeida Theatre in Islington and is honorary consultant at The Royal College of Art. We acknowledge with gratitude that John Wiley & Sons allowed us to reprint this article in the present book.

Lastly, I should like to thank my family: my children, who have shown me how young people grow up, something that no amount of training could have done, and my wife, Sonja, for her example and her support.

# 1

# Introduction

*'I am nobody, therefore I should have no body' (a female patient with Anorexia Nervosa).*

## Stigma and Eating Disorders

### Patient A

*A man of 34 with a 15-year history of Anorexia Nervosa had spent only a few months during that time out of hospital. He was attempting to maintain his weight in the community and required some social work assistance not available via the eating disorders service. A referral to the Community Mental Health Team (CMHT) manager was met with rejection on the grounds that the patient did not have a 'severe and enduring mental illness'.*

This experience led to the author introducing the term severe and enduring eating disorder (SEED) (Robinson, 2006a). Having worked for many years with patients as well as their families, struggling with the effects of prolonged eating disorders, it was very clear to me that they could be severe, often life threatening and requiring hospital care, and as the case above exemplifies, they could go on for a very long time, so the 'severe and enduring' label, which, in the United Kingdom, is a ticket to community mental health services, was apposite. In that case, an explanation led to the patient being taken on and helped, and the case is not meant to show that such patients are frequently neglected by services. However, sometimes they are, and the

*Severe and Enduring Eating Disorder*   Paul Robinson
© 2009 John Wiley & Sons, Ltd

reaction reflects a number of feelings about people with eating disorders shared by both the public and helping professions. Crisp (2000) in a survey of public views found that about one-third of people believed that individuals with eating disorders could pull themselves together, have only themselves to blame and would be hard to talk to. However, this group of citizens were quite optimistic (overly so) about prognosis (90% thought that the outcome would be favourable). Amongst health care professionals, it is not uncommon to find a curious mixture of views. Some appear to believe that eating disorders are trivial, that they are suffered only by silly rich girls trying to diet and emulate glossy magazine icons. On other occasions, the same people may view eating disorders as so serious and complex that all must be treated by a specialist service. As in all extreme views, they both contain an element of truth. Some girls with anorexia or bulimia nervosa do, indeed, come from well-off families, and live in an atmosphere in which the culture of thinness predominates, although that does not mean that their illnesses are trivial. Secondly, some people with eating disorders do suffer from very severe and dangerous illness and require specialist help. Health workers sometimes, in addition, hold an admixture of other views which reduce the chances that they will agree to engage with someone with an eating disorder. The first is that the patient is to blame for the illness. There appears to be a spectrum of belief about responsibility, with accompanying attitudes, well illustrated in Crisp's study, so that in some disorders, such as dementia, the patient is largely exonerated from blame for the illness and is treated as having developed a brain disease completely beyond his control. Such a patient (in this world view) merits the greatest degree of sympathy. In the middle of the spectrum are people whose behaviour or personality may have contributed to the illness. Patients with severe depression are in this category, with half the population believing that they can 'pull themselves together' (Crisp, 2000).

In the world of physical medicine, someone with lung cancer due to lifelong heavy smoking, someone with pneumonia who is HIV positive due to sexual transmission of the virus and someone very overweight with diabetes mellitus may be victims of prejudice. Some surgeons have suggested that people who continue to drink should not be given liver transplants, and those who continue to smoke should not be offered some forms of arterial surgery unless they agree to quit (Powell and Greenhalgh, 1994), and many would concur that this is justifiable.

At the far end of the spectrum lie patients who are deemed to be 'doing it to themselves'. In this sorry group are people with eating disorders, personality disorders and addictions. Interestingly, the Mental Health Act, which suggests that perhaps individuals are not completely responsible for

| Minimal blame | Moderate blame | Major blame |
|---|---|---|

I———————————————————————————————I

| Alzheimer's | Depression | Addictions |
| Epilepsy | Schizophrenia | Personality disorder |
| Learning difficulties / brain damage | Phobias | Eating disorders |

**Figure 1.1** The blame spectrum of mental disorders

their behaviour, can apply to the first two, but not the last set of conditions. Patients with severe eating disorders have been targets of such comments as 'she's running me round in circles while I have a ward of real patients to treat' (consultant psychiatrist). Personality disorder elicits such negative attitudes from psychiatrists that it has been proposed that the term be abandoned (Lewis and Appleby, 1988). When patients on psychiatric wards cause problems it is sometimes concluded that the problem is either 'caused by illness' or 'behavioural'. The former descriptor implies that a behaviour, such as violence, is a symptom of illness, such as schizophrenia, and probably not completely under the patient's control. The latter term 'behavioural' implies that the problem is not due to mental illness and is under at least some voluntary control. The distinction may have some validity with the former types of behaviour responding better to medication and attention, and the latter types to withdrawal of attention. The problem with the distinction is the stigma that it implies, with some patients being more worthy than others. Descriptors such as 'manipulative' and 'hysterical' have become less prevalent probably because of their negative connotations, to be replaced by successor terms associated with personality disorder. The stigmatization of people at the 'only themselves to blame' end of the blame spectrum (see Figure 1.1) may well be a reflection of health workers' anxiety that they themselves will be blamed by the institution if the patient does do something extreme. The blame culture in the NHS has, unfortunately, outlived its obituarists (Wise, 2001; National Audit Office, 2005).

## Severe and Enduring?

Psychological problems are very common, while resources for treatment of mental disorders are limited. Providers of services have therefore, rightly, been encouraged to concentrate on mental disorders that can be described as severe and enduring, at the expense of the far more numerous psychological difficulties that are, by contrast, relatively less severe and sometimes self-limiting. There has been a concern that services might be directed towards these latter groups for a number of reasons. Firstly, they are more common, secondly, they are probably more able to present themselves for help (and even demand it), and thirdly, because they are more like 'us' they are likely to be easier and more rewarding to treat. If we accept that the first call on our scarce resources should be by individuals in the severe and enduring category (SEMI: severe and enduring mental illness) there remains substantial confusion, evident in the CMHT response which opened this chapter. GPs have also indicated that they are unsure as to the boundaries of the term (Barr, 2001). One common interpretation is to equate SEMI with chronic schizophrenic or depressive psychosis. This would clearly be over-restrictive and risks depriving people with equally debilitating obsessive compulsive disorder or Anorexia Nervosa of necessary help from mental health professionals. Holloway (2005) regards schizophrenia as the paradigm of severe mental illness, while he adds 'other mental disorders whose social functioning is significantly affected by their illness or disorder (which will include some people with a diagnosis of depressive illness, obsessive-compulsive disorder and personality disorder)'. Anorexia Nervosa, which has a standardized mortality rate of around 10.5 times the norm (Birmingham *et al.*, 2005), is not included, although the implication is that it could have a place.

The 'severe and enduring' descriptor seems to have originated in the National Service Framework (NSF) for mental health, published in 1999. Introducing the term, the NSF gives us some help in its interpretation:

**p46**

*People with recurrent or severe and enduring mental illness, for example schizophrenia, bipolar affective disorder or organic mental disorder, severe anxiety disorders or severe eating disorders, have complex needs which may require the continuing care of specialist mental health services working effectively with other agencies. Most people manage well with this care and benefit from living in the community, posing no risk to themselves or others (Department of Health, 1999a).*

The intention appears to have been to include all people with mental disorder whose disorder is disabling and long lasting, whatever it is. Many patients with chronic anorexia and bulimia nervosa have problems which accord with this definition.

# How Severe, How Enduring?

This book is about serious illness in people who have problems in mental, physical, occupational, social and family domains. The concept of severity is certainly relevant. It is a complex one, however. BMI on its own is not a particularly reliable marker of illness. A 16-year-old whose weight falls from a BMI of 20 to 15 in 6 months may be mortally ill. In contrast, a 40-year-old who has been at a BMI of 13 for 15 years may be working. For the 16-year-old, the clinical priorities may be as follows:

1. Saving her life.
2. Helping her improve her nutrition.
3. Engaging her and her family in therapy to help her get back to a healthy weight as soon as possible.
4. Continuing therapeutic work to help her avoid relapses.

The 40-year-old may have completely different priorities:

1. Maintaining the maximum possible level of nutritional health.
2. Managing crises, medical or psychological.
3. Keeping at work.
4. Maintaining social contacts.
5. Providing care for an elderly, ailing parent.
6. Addressing complications of her eating disorder such as osteoporosis.
7. Dealing with depression.

We have two groups of patients therefore, the acutely ill young patient with a short history of Anorexia Nervosa and not much else and the chronically ill patient with a long history of Anorexia Nervosa with physical, psychological and social complications. The acronym SEED applies only to the latter.

Consider this case:

### Patient B

*A 20-year-old woman presents with a 4-year history of severe weight loss and depression. During inpatient treatment for her malnutrition, her depression becomes worse and she reports hearing derogatory voices. By this time, she has been in hospital for 4 months. She is given ECT and improves, but during treatment for a leg spasm by epidural analgesia, she develops bilateral paralysis of her legs. She is in a medical and a neurological ward for a year, and gradually improves enough to return to the eating disorders ward. She recovers memories of sexual abuse, and over the following 3 years makes a good recovery.*

This illness was certainly severe (it nearly killed her) and it did endure for about 8 years. One could argue that her case should be included in the SEED category, even though she eventually recovered. One of the most remarkable aspects of treating eating disorders is that patients do, against all predictions, sometimes recover after 8, 10 and even 20 years of illness. The above case also raises the question of the boundaries of eating disorders. Did she have several illnesses or only one? Consider the case of tuberculosis (TB), before the causative bacterium was discovered. A patient might consult the doctor with a cough, with weight loss and fever, with red swellings on his legs, and even with epilepsy and personality change. Until the discovery of the bacillus, these diverse manifestations of TB could well have been thought to be caused by different processes. When the bug was discovered, and found to be lurking in the tissues of all people with these problems, they were all seen as manifestations of the same disease, TB.

In psychiatry, we largely occupy a world in which the bug has yet to be discovered. In Anorexia Nervosa it could be so many things, and most likely be a combination of several. Even in TB the bug is not the whole story. Someone infected would only actually get the disease if one or more other processes, including poverty, malnutrition (including Anorexia Nervosa) and weakness of the immune system, such as that caused by AIDS, are present. The bug is necessary but not sufficient. In Anorexia Nervosa predisposing factors such as an eating disorder in the family have been identified, but none might be essential. It is possible that, if there are 10 contributors to the disorder, 4 of them might be contributory in one patient and another 4 might together lead to the disorder in a second patient. In the patient described above (she reappears in more detail in Chapter 2), the course of the illness suggested strongly that the abuse she suffered in her adolescence was key to the development of her illness. If that is true (it is very difficult to be absolutely sure), then all problems of this patient were probably caused by it. This includes Anorexia Nervosa, psychotic depression and conversion disorder (hysterical paralysis). By analogy with infectious disease, if we have the putative causative agent (sexual abuse) then all manifestations of illness caused by it are part of the same disease.

SEED, therefore, may contain diverse clinical spectra. It can be stable, with continuing ill health for many years, but there is little change in the disorder, except that produced by chronic complications. Patients with long-standing stable eating disorders in whom the illness has been continuously present for a minimum time are the group who merit the descriptor SEED. The length of time chosen is to some extent arbitrary. Steinhausen (2002) found that recovery continued to occur after 10 years of illness, although the rate appeared to be slowing when compared to 4–10 years. Ten years is by any definition a long illness, and problems associated with chronicity are likely to occur at that stage. While research which gives better guidance is awaited, I suggest that 10 years be adopted as the minimum duration of continuous disorder for SEED. The majority of patients with SEED will be underweight, and therefore fulfil criteria for Anorexia Nervosa. There will, however, be variation, and any eating disorder can be severe and long lasting enough to merit inclusion in the SEED category. SEED can therefore, if necessary, be suffixed according to the eating disorder from which the patient is suffering, i.e. SEED-AN, SEED-BN, SEED-BED, etc.

Another group of patients with a very unstable disorder, such as Patient B described above, but with a duration that may not extend to 10 years, should perhaps be identified as they require such extensive and expensive treatment. These patients could be labelled as having severe and unstable eating disorder. The group would include patients requiring prolonged and/or frequent hospital admissions for life-threatening clinical problems including undernutrition, electrolyte disturbance, depression, psychosis, suicidal and other self-harming behaviours and substance misuse.

Yager (2007) draws our attention to the distinction between treatment non-response, when the patient accepts treatments offered, and treatment reluctance, when compliance and engagement are lacking. He rightly points to motivation and its enhancement as key to management of chronic eating disorders.

## Severity

How severe should a patient's illness be to merit the SEED attribution? A strict definition is one that comes from the NSF: the patient has 'complex needs which (may) require the continuing care of specialist mental health services working effectively with other agencies'. A definition focused on symptoms would be:

*A patient with symptoms of an eating disorder which interfere substantially with quality of life.*

The eventual definition of SEED will require a large study of patients with long-term eating disorders in which measure of physical and psychological symptoms, as well as quality of life, adaptation to illness, social consequences and use of services among others, would be made.

## Assessment of a Patient with Chronic Stable SEED

How should the assessment of such a patient be approached? Her problems originate with nutritional disturbance, but certainly do not end there. It is worth giving a little thought to a system within which to assess an individual's difficulties and needs.

The Care Programme Approach (Department of Health, 1990, 1999b) gives detailed guidance on provision of care to people with SEMI, citing the following domains (see Table 1.1) as examples of those that might require attention:

1. Physical health
2. Mental health
3. Social and Family
4. Housing
5. Finance
6. Occupation (employment, education).

These domains will be used to inform the content of this book, and a proposed format for CPA documentation will be provided.

In addition to the domains, the following areas need to be addressed:

1. A list of names and contact details of professionals responsible for the delivery of the Care Programme.
2. The name and contact details of a key worker/care coordinator.
3. The name and contact details of a carer, if possible.
4. The formulation of a care plan and regular review.
5. The identification of signs of relapse or increasing risk.

**Table 1.1** Domains and handicaps in SEED

| Domains | Primary handicaps | Secondary handicaps |
| --- | --- | --- |
| Physical | Inability to climb stairs | Chronically poor health |
| | Poor sleep | Social isolation |
| | Risk of death | |
| | Fractures | |
| | Exercise abuse | |
| Psychological | Poor motivation (depression) | Social isolation |
| | Time management problems (OCD) | Home care poor |
| | Hoarding | Self-neglect |
| Social | Inability to eat in public | Social isolation |
| | Difficulty maintaining relationships | |
| | Stigma | |
| Family | Family conflict | Alienation from or overdependence on family |
| | Family exhaustion | |
| Housing | Relapse when living alone | Frequent readmissions Confirmed in sick role |
| Finance | Difficulty spending | Poor home environment Social isolation |
| Occupation | Difficulty working | Reduced social contact |

## Handicap and Adaptation (See Figure 1.2 )

The concept of handicap has long been used to help characterize the difficulties faced by people with physical illness such as polio, mental illness such as schizophrenia and learning difficulties. It is useful because it can be applied to any of the domains listed above. Moreover, a symptom such as difficulty eating in public, which might cause a major handicap to one person, may not cause much problem to another. The difference may reside, not in the symptom itself, but in other areas such as social support, personality and occupation. It is perhaps more helpful to talk about adaptation, because the word has positive connotations, handicap representing the half-empty glass and adaptation its more optimistic half-full complement. Adaptation

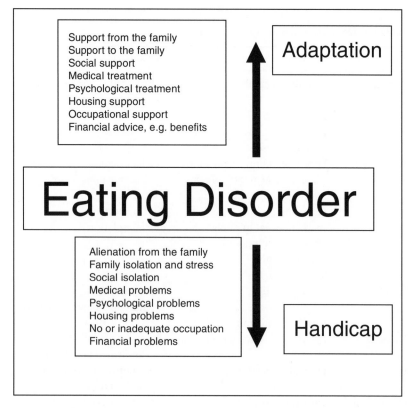

**Figure 1.2** Adaptation and handicap in mental disorder.

is the end result of the specific symptom, the individual's reaction to it and the influences of society to both. Services provided to the patient need to minimize handicap and maximize adaptation.

Let us consider a person with SEED:

*Patient C is aged 32 and began to lose weight in her late teens. Repeated attempts at treatment were inevitably followed by rapid relapse, but after the age of 25 she maintained a low but stable BMI of 14.2, thereby avoiding further hospitalizations. However, she continued to have problems in many areas: she had difficulty getting to her flat on the fourth floor of a house with no lift; she spent several hours each morning cleaning her flat in a ritualistic way; she had virtually no social life; and she was on long-term sick leave from her job as a bank clerk.*

Patient C has difficulties in a number of domains. She has problems in physical health (muscle weakness), mental health (obsessive compulsive cleaning), social function (isolation), housing (too many stairs), finance (especially if she is unable to keep her job) and occupation (her own confidence at work, attitudes of employers). Many of these problems could be addressed if she improved her nutritional state. However, she has shown that she is not able to adapt to a higher weight, and while we may wish to encourage weight gain, we should not anticipate it, and our interventions in the different domains need to be designed with the expectation that her weight will stay around the same. These interventions could extend into a wide variety of psychological, psychiatric, social and other fields. From the nutritional point of view, while weight gain might be a no-no, it would be worth checking her blood count, which could reveal anaemia, treatable with iron or vitamin B12. Her obsessive compulsive disorder (OCD) is most likely integral to her eating disorder, related to both starvation (which tends to produce OCD symptoms (Keys *et al.*, 1950)) and a drive to over-exercise. If we accept that her eating disorder is stable, these are unlikely to change. However, cognitive behaviour therapy including exposure and response prevention, established as effective treatment for OCD without an eating disorder (National Collaborating Centre for Mental Health, 2005), could be tried, especially if Patient C is desperate to reduce her cleaning rituals. Moreover, an SSRI (selective serotonin re-uptake inhibition) antidepressant could also be offered as an effective intervention in OCD. Moving onto psychosocial interventions, social isolation could be addressed in a number of ways, including activities such as classes or voluntary work and therapy or self-help groups which may or may not be eating disorder focused. Rehousing with fewer stairs might be considered, while at work she might be encouraged to question her employer's handling of her case, especially if she can be shown to perform her role adequately in spite of her long-standing eating disorder.

The overall aims would be to reduce symptoms, both physical and psychological, as far as possible, given presently available interventions and to maximize adaptation to the residual problems, and so minimize handicap.

## The Sick Role: Institutionalization

Hirsch (1976) suggested that people with schizophrenia had three types of handicap with which to contend:

*Primary handicap.* The effects of the illness itself.

*Secondary handicap.* The effects of being in the role of a psychiatric patient over many years; relevant factors being the patient's ability to deal with the outside world, his attitude to himself and others and the attitudes of family, employer and the public.

*Premorbid handicap.* Factors that contribute to the onset of illness, such as the personality structure, poverty, poor education, and poor employment opportunities.

Can this approach be adapted for people with eating disorders? The primary handicap would encompass the effects of all the psychological, physical and social problems that comprise eating disorders and the commonly associated disorders such as depression and OCD. In the context of schizophrenia, secondary handicap was often seen as being caused due to long periods spent in hospital, with the associated infantilization of the patient and increasing dependence on the institution, resulting in patients having great difficulty leaving the hospital at the time of discharge. Since the closure of the large mental hospitals, secondary handicap has been recognized as accompanying any long-term mental illness, as a result of the combination of the symptoms (e.g. hearing voices, depression) and the resulting problems of chronicity. Schizophrenia often results in impaired relationships and social engagement. A constellation of difficulties frequently observed is as follows.

*The patient feels persecuted, may behave in an odd manner, the public avoid him resulting in progressive isolation, and increasing alienation, including loss of employment and exclusion/withdrawal from social settings.*

The stigma associated with eating disorders is different from that accompanying schizophrenia, in that patients are less likely to be perceived as dangerous (Crisp, 2000). People with eating disorders, especially Anorexia Nervosa, often do suffer from social isolation, however. In them, the constellation is more likely to be as follows.

*The patient feels uncomfortable eating out and therefore misses many social engagements. Other people are dismayed by the patient's appearance and do not know how to help or even bring up the subject of her emaciation. The patient's opportunities for social interaction progressively diminish. Her appearance and her hormonal deficiency state make romantic encounters less likely. Her physical appearance may lead employers to judge her too ill to work, and to regard her as unsuitable because of the possible impact on customers and colleagues. Moreover, colleagues' suspicions that she may be bingeing or purging at work can lead to alienation in the workplace.*

The secondary handicaps of eating disorders can, like the domains, be divided into physical, psychological, social, family, housing and occupational. Taking Hirsch's definition, the key characteristic of a secondary handicap is that it is an effect of having been in the sick role for a number of years. It should be distinguished from a late symptom. For example, a patient who develops Anorexia Nervosa at the age of 20, then has a fracture of the spine due to osteoporosis at 40, has a symptom of the Anorexia Nervosa which has appeared late in the disorder. However, that same patient may have become socially isolated over the 20 years of illness and have lost her job as a result of new management who regarded her as physically too weak to continue.

## Models of Illness: Many Hats on One Head

There is an unfortunate tendency in mental health to adopt one model of illness to the exclusion of others. It is sometimes argued that to allow more than one model into one's thinking encourages sloppiness and that an individual should stick to one way of approaching clinical problems. Hence, there are battles between so-called organic, psychodynamic and cognitive behavioural schools all convinced, like religious fundamentalists, that they have the right view. However, they are more like the blind men of Indostan grasping different parts of the elephant and concluding that the animal was like the part they had touched:

*Each in his own opinion*
*Exceeding stiff and strong,*
*Though each was partly in the right,*
*And all were in the wrong!*

There are numerous ways to look at human behaviour, each way characterized by a different context. Different clinical situations demand different approaches; a few of which follow.

## Psychodynamic or Psychoanalytic Approach

Many of the concepts elaborated by Freud and his successors are extremely valuable thinking aids in approaching eating disorders. The patient with Anorexia Nervosa is engaged in a non-verbal communication which, deciphered, says, 'I cannot feed myself or be responsible for looking after my own health.' This suggests regression to a very early stage, before the infant can feed herself. Ideas derived from a variety of psychoanalytic strands are in regular usage in attempts to make sense of eating disorders. Some of the most compelling are those of object relations and attachment theories. These theories posit the importance of primary relationships in the development of the infant and young person. The range of developmental considerations that have impacted on psychotherapeutic models have been well reviewed by Fonagy and Target (2003). Consider the following case history:

*Patient D was the child of a mother who was chronically depressed. At 13 she passed through puberty and by 14 she had developed Anorexia Nervosa. In both individual and family therapy, there was evidence that she had not made a strong emotional connection with her mother and she began to relate to other adults, her father, doctors, nurses, entirely through the medium of her eating disorder. After many hospital admissions, she married a man with an obsession with fitness, and continued her eating disordered behaviour, with food restriction and over-exercise. Her relationship with her husband was dominated by her eating disorder. He attended her every meal, and made sure she ate a full diet. She managed to continue weight loss by means of over-exercising, and this led to frequent tension between them. She was referred to a day hospital in which she was given the choice to either lose weight and be admitted once again to hospital or maintain it and work on her issues. She found this approach very challenging and indicated that she felt more comfortable with a more authoritarian approach that she could resist. She communicated in therapy that she had never been close to any individual and that only through her eating disorder, which resulted in conflict with other individuals who usually tried to force her to eat, had she had any form of emotional relationship, albeit a negative one.*

The object relations approach was, for her, helpful and relevant. She had never developed an emotional bond with any individual in her life, for reasons that can be conjectured, but not fully understood. She thus lacked substantial internal objects (i.e. an internal mother, father, lover, etc.) which, had they developed, might have supported her and allowed her to deal with the demands of loneliness, criticism, others' need for care, etc. In their absence, however, she substituted anorexic behaviour for internal objects resulting in relationships with others in which she was the dependent, demanding child and others always placed in the carer role, absolved of the need to care for others. She addressed (but did not satisfy) her dependency needs and became stuck at an infantile level of social development.

This formulation also suggests an approach to treatment which can be adopted by all staff. Therapeutic relationships should be supportive, but behaviour which perpetuates the regressed role should be challenged. Her therapy need not be psychoanalytic, although it could be. The insights provided by the analytic approach can inform all meetings with staff and help edge Patient D towards a more adult way of relating.

## Cognitive and Behavioural Approaches

CBT is often placed as the more evidence-based alternative to analytic therapy and there is no doubt about its helpfulness in many clinical situations. The insights of CBT can also be extremely useful in other therapeutic activities, not generally thought of as CBT, for example supportive individual therapy and family therapy. Patient D's dilemma could well be presented by looking at her attitudes to herself including her body image, her deeply held beliefs (schemas) about herself as someone who could never be independent and who would always be a failure, her behaviour such as her food restriction, her repeated and obsessive exercising and her constant examination of her body parts in the mirror. The interactions between her beliefs and her behaviours reinforce each other and perpetuate the anorexic lifestyle. Fundamental beliefs about the self are, of course, commonly encountered in psychoanalytic formulations, as are many other 'CBT' concepts such as generalization and personalization.

Many of the differences between schools of therapy are to do with packaging and marketing. Like Scottish kilts, in which there is a wide variety of patterns from the different clans (some of whom will not talk to each other) all at least cover the essentials. So many of the concepts are either labelled differently in each approach, or used without being attributed by therapists. It often seems that the packaging of a therapy serves the individuals who are building their careers by promoting a particular named therapy, more than the patients who are the presumed beneficiaries. This may, however, be too harsh, and the packages, whether psychodynamic, CBT or newer ones such as dialectical behaviour therapy (DBT) (Linehan, 1993) or mentalization-based therapy (MBT) (Bateman and Fonagy, 2004) may well provide a therapy with practical and theoretical coherence, better than eclectic approaches that try to take from all.

## Biological Approaches

Psychiatrists sometimes characterize themselves or are described by others as 'biological' or 'psychosocial' in orientation. Indeed, psychiatry departments in US medical schools accrue similar labels. In the 1970s, most US departments were psychoanalytic in orientation and in the 1980s many changed to biological schools. What does the term imply? At its most extreme, it can be a deterministic set of beliefs that holds that all behaviour, including mental symptoms, is predetermined by the molecular configuration of the individual, and that psychosocial interventions merely act as additional molecular influences that make changes in the patient's chemistry and hence modify behaviour.

More usually, the term implies a belief that the most important influences which lead to psychiatric presentation are biological. The range of such influences is wide. Genetic factors are extremely important, so that the possession of a set of genes that predispose to Anorexia Nervosa is said to explain most of the patient's anorexic symptoms. In addition, chemical changes in the brain which might be partly genetically determined, but which might also arise as a result of environmental influences, are held to be of great importance. In psychiatric disorder few such changes have been conclusively identified, and many of them are inferred because certain drugs with common actions (e.g. raising serotonin levels or blocking the action of dopamine) have therapeutic effects on certain conditions (respectively depression and psychosis). This partly explains why 'biological' psychiatrists often turn to medication to help the patient. Thirdly, physical changes, for example in brain structure, are held to account for behavioural change. This is evident in a patient with advanced Alzheimer's disease but may also be posited in someone with schizophrenia who has been found to have a slight reduction in brain tissue, possibly deriving from birth trauma. In the eating disorders field, a physiological change which has been suggested as perpetuating undereating in Anorexia Nervosa by increasing fullness after meals is delayed gastric emptying. This change, which probably occurs secondary to undereating, is thought to cause prolonged gastric discomfort after meals which inhibits further eating (Robinson, 1989).

The sad thing about the tendency to be attached to one model is that most models are useful and complementary. Just as physics and chemistry, each has something different and relevant to say about the same natural phenomenon; psychodynamic, cognitive behavioural, biological and other models of behaviour all have useful ideas to contribute to the understanding of human behaviour. A holistic approach in which each level of the system is examined using the most appropriate tools could lead to a formulation with developmental, psychodynamic, cognitive, behavioural and systemic dimensions, each contributing to a comprehensive view of the problem.

## Systemic Approaches

Because systemic approaches purport to include all elements in a system, they have the potential to address the above complaint. In practice, systemic views tend to look at the way elements relate to each other, rather like a satellite picture of an archipelago. The elements in question can be individuals in a family, or in a therapeutic system (e.g. patient, eating disorders team, community mental health team, family), or even ways of viewing the problem (such as a biological and a social model). These ideas are very useful for understanding tensions within the different systems, and discerning why things might be going wrong:

### Patient E

*A patient who was physically abused by her father before he left the family home becomes very close to her mother. In treatment for severe depression and an eating disorder, she forms a close relationship with a female therapist. The male psychiatrist's opinion that the patient requires electro-convulsive therapy for her psychotic depression is strongly resisted by the therapist. Aside from the complex clinical and ethical issues about treatment, the mirroring of the patient's relationship with her parents by the relationship with team members is important to identify, especially as it could lead to a serious rift within the team.*

Complexity theory is another useful tool in the difficult task of bringing together the numerous influences that bear on clinical, and especially psychiatric, problems. Strange attractors are high-level mathematical functions that can say something about the behaviour of complex systems. They have been used to study weather patterns, and economic systems, and have been applied to human behaviour, including therapeutic systems (Robertson and Combs, 1995). The idea that there could be a formula which could reflect what is going on in a family or other system is, in itself, quite helpful. The theoretical attractor 'restricting Anorexia Nervosa' would have quite powerful organizing influences on a family system and these would be very different from those of another theoretical attractor 'bulimic Anorexia Nervosa' which would be rather more chaotic. The attractor 'borderline PD with eating disorder' could be a particularly chaotic function.

Another interesting and useful concept within complexity theory is fractal theory, in which complex systems are found to repeat similar patterns at many levels of magnification. Thus, regular fluctuations in serotonin levels could be associated with mood fluctuations, and, at a behavioural level, oscillating bingeing or self-harming behaviour. In a couple, closeness and distance in the relationship could well oscillate to the same wave and, in the therapeutic system, the frequency and intensity of interventions might be similarly oscillating to the same equation. A rather odd example of a possible fractal structure is represented by the effects of anticonvulsants in stabilizing membranes, reducing abnormal electrical discharges and suppressing epileptic attacks (all presumably causally linked). The same drugs, in an action which appears to leap neuro-organizational levels, also stabilize mood and behaviour in patients with bipolar or borderline personality disorder. The actions of the drugs at four different levels of the system have in common the smoothing of chaotic patterns.

# 2

# SEED, Psychiatric Considerations

Patients are usually not avid readers of the DSM-IV (1994), nor of the ICD-10 (World Health Organization, 1992), and their symptoms therefore do not fall neatly into the constructs that committees make for them. If a psychiatrist makes Diagnosis A, but is also found to have B, then the latter is often called 'co-morbidity'. Thus, for the eating disorder specialist, affective disorder, obsessive compulsive disorder, drug misuse and personality disorder are seen as co-morbid conditions to the main condition, the eating disorder. For the substance misuse psychiatrist, an eating disorder is seen as co-morbid to the main or primary condition, the drug problem. Sometimes, in a patient suffering from several conditions, the one that is called 'primary' is the one for which there are better local services, or, more worryingly, the one that is dealt with by someone else.

Real patients, however, have the experiences they have, and any professional attempting to use the existing diagnostic system will have found often that it is a Procrustean bed[1] which poorly serves the actual customers. In the group of patients we are considering, those with longstanding problems, the difficulties tend to mount with time, and diagnoses multiply. The list of psychiatric diagnoses can include depression, anxiety, drug misuse and addiction, obsessive compulsive disorder and borderline personality disorder. In this chapter, a number of case histories will be presented in order to

---

[1] *Procrustes* was a mythical bandit from Attica. He had an iron bed into which he invited every passerby to lie down. If the guest proved too tall, he would amputate the excess length; if the victim was found too short, he was then stretched out on the rack until he fit. Nobody would ever fit in the bed because it was secretly adjustable. (Wikipedia).

---

*Severe and Enduring Eating Disorder*    Paul Robinson
© 2009 John Wiley & Sons, Ltd

illustrate the range of symptoms encountered. Some of these can be traced back to the inception of the eating disorder, some to effects of the physical changes accompanying the eating disorder, some to chronicity and some to treatment. Management of patients with severe SEED can be extremely challenging, and include interventions at many levels of the system. At the biological level, interventions aimed at helping the patient modify weight and nutrition, as well as chemicals to shift brain neurotransmitters are available, while behaviourally, psychological therapies can give the patient the skills to avoid self-damaging and unhelpful behaviours. This level also includes milieu therapy, such as that provided in a high-quality psychiatric inpatient service, providing protection, asylum and nurturing. At the social level, family interventions can encourage change in the way families interact around the symptoms, while in the wider social context, supported housing, training and education and voluntary and paid work may all be appropriate and useful. Looking specifically at medical, milieu and psychological therapies offered to patients with SEED, the range is diverse:

1. *Establishing a therapeutic relationship.* The patient establishes trusting relationships with staff members and creates new object relations which foster different and more functional associations with present and future people in her life.
2. *Specific psychological therapies.* The patient learns new ways of dealing with thoughts and emotions which accompany difficulties in relationships and other experiences.
3. *Non-verbal therapies.* The patient explores alternative languages to that of self-damaging behaviour in order to express distress.
4. *Family approaches.* The patient and her family explore alternative ways of communication about their difficulties.
5. *Intensive care therapy.* The patient is, if possible, prevented from harming herself by constant nursing and legal constraints on her self-damaging behaviour.
6. *Nutritional therapy.* The patient is provided with dietetic advice, and sometimes meals which may be in a structured environment and helped to achieve realistic nutritional goals.
7. *Pharmacological interventions.* The patient is provided with drugs (or ECT) which suppress certain powerful thoughts and emotions so that others can have a chance of taking their place.

This list is not exhaustive, but includes a fair proportion of the interventions used in such patients. It will be noted that some of them apply to patients who are acutely unwell, usually requiring hospital care to keep them alive.

## Symptoms of SEED Attributable to Malnutrition and Body Image Disturbance

*Nutritional symptoms in patients with SEED*

The patient with a long-term, severe eating disorder, at or below the normal weight range, is grappling with two opposing sets of demands on her body. One set concerns aspects of physiology and behaviour that favour survival in the face of diminished availability of food, and no doubt have arisen by natural selection in the course of evolution.

*Behaviours favouring food location and consumption*    The patient may be thinking constantly about food, even dreaming about it. She may take a profound interest in other people's eating, prepare food for them, which she may insist that they consume. Obesity in pet cats and dogs is not unknown due to overfeeding by their eating disordered owners. Interest in food may take the form of embarking on a career in the catering or hospitality industries. This symptom appears to be related to food deprivation, and this in patients takes two main forms: short-term and long-term. Short-term deprivation occurs when a patient drastically reduces her food intake on a particular day. She can manage to get through the day, eating 'healthy food' (i.e. of almost no nutritional value) and when evening comes, she may be increasingly agitated. In patients with bulimia nervosa, or Anorexia Nervosa, bulimic subtype, this is when bingeing is likely to occur, and can be seen as a healthy response to food deprivation. Short-term food deprivation is seen in patients with both Anorexia Nervosa and in most with bulimia nervosa. In overweight patients with binge eating disorder, it is often seen when the patient is attempting to diet strictly, and a proportion of binges in such patients can be seen as due to deprivation. Long-term deprivation occurs when a patient's net calorie intake is low enough to produce weight loss. This is seen, of course in Anorexia Nervosa, but also in bulimia nervosa in which weight loss is not severe enough to reduce BMI below the normal range, or to produce amenorrhoea. It seems that the combination of short-term and long-term deprivation seen moderately in BN and severely in AN lead to the most distressing preoccupations with food, and in a proportion of patients, to bingeing behaviour. This is compatible with set point theory of weight control, which, although controversial, has in its favour a fair amount of supporting evidence (Harris, 1990). This mechanism, therefore, appears to be related to food preoccupation and bingeing in patients with eating disorders.

While not increasing nutritional intake, the starving individual will be found to chew non-nutritional objects such as wood, and to take salt, vinegar and other condiments in order to stimulate the taste and chewing part of the nutritional process. This behaviour has only limited effect on hunger and food seeking, which is what would be expected, as it does not solve the body's nutritional deprivation state.

*Behaviours favouring food conservation*    Three main symptoms common in patients with eating disorders seem to serve this mechanism, namely eking behaviours, postprandial enhanced satiety and hoarding. Eking behaviours occur in starved individuals, whatever the cause. Food is stretched as far as it will go, by being cut up small, eaten extremely slowly and chewed interminably, all of which are seen in eating disorders. In the mind of the patient, these behaviours also favour decreased food intake when there is plenty around. However, the behaviours presumably developed in evolution at a time when food was scarce and eking was helpful. Hoarding is of course observed in squirrels, preparing for the winter. In patients with eating disorders it can be quite dramatic. One patient was visited at home, and was found to have been hoarding dozens of tins of food, all stolen from supermarkets, which filled an entire room. All the tins were unopened. Lastly, enhanced satiety is most likely closely related to delayed gastric emptying, seen in Anorexia Nervosa and probably due to undereating, as it reverses with two weeks of normal food intake (Robinson, Barrett and Clarke, 1988). At first, delayed gastric emptying seems contrary to natural selection as it could be seen to favour undereating, as it may do in Anorexia Nervosa. However, in times of food shortage it lengthens the time between ingestion and metabolism, allowing the stomach to be used as a food store (or larder) and reducing the rate at which nutrients, especially protein which does not have extensive storage sites, are used up.

*Behaviours favouring energy conservation*    Underactivity, seen in starved non-eating disordered individuals, is often absent in eating disorders, and patients may maximize their energy expenditure by overexercising. However, depression, a very common symptom, could be seen as favouring social withdrawal as can hyposexuality. Moreover, amenorrhoea is clearly energy conserving, protecting the starved individual from the energy demands of pregnancy and lactation. Thyroid function in Anorexia Nervosa is also depressed, favouring a reduction in energy expenditure. This adaptive hypothyroidism should not be treated with thyroid hormone replacement.

### *Behaviours attributable to body image disturbance in SEED*

The second set of forces operating on the patient concerns her psychologically mediated body image needs. These can be summarized as follows.

*Avoiding eating*   In direct conflict with the biological imperative to eat, the patient has an entire complex of thoughts and feelings which directly oppose it. Thus, although she is aware of the intense urge to eat, she also harbours equally powerful thoughts proscribing or limiting eating. These are, of course, linked to her belief and her perception of herself as overweight, the body image distortion. While this belief appears to have the characteristics of a delusion, as it is false, unshakeably held and is not shared by the rest of society, most psychiatrists believe it to be an *overvalued idea*, different from the delusions of, say, schizophrenia. Indeed, some patients with psychosis can have delusions about their bodies, such as a belief that the stomach has disappeared, that there is no mouth, or that the abdomen is infested by worms. The body image distortion seen in Anorexia Nervosa may be extreme, but is usually not quite as bizarre as those encountered in psychosis. The beliefs are reflected in a harsh and cynical maxim enunciated by the then Duchess of Windsor, Wallis Simpson, 'You can never be too rich or too thin!' The second form of body image distortion is body disparagement, that is, intense criticism or hatred of parts of the body, which commonly include thighs, hips, arms, face and breasts. These thoughts, although somewhat less extreme, also lead the patient to feel that she is too large and needs to reduce weight by whatever means possible. They are encountered in patients with both anorexia and bulimia nervosa. These thoughts lead to a secondary belief that only certain foods, with low calories, such as salad, are acceptable, and ingestion of anything else leads to guilt, shame and a determination to get rid of the ingested calories. Gastric fullness exacerbates this process by convincing the patient that as she feels full, she must have overeaten, and is therefore greedy, and also that her stomach is protruding. The gastric emptying delay, mentioned above, which may increase the efficiency of digestion, also serves to increase the feeling of fullness and hence the guilt and self-criticism. Moreover, gastric sensations may be experienced as correlating with negative emotional experiences, such as sadness or fatness, a process that has been termed *paraceptivity* (Robinson, 1989). The fuller the patient's stomach, the more sad, fat or anxious she may feel, and these emotional states can be seen to diminish as the stomach becomes more empty during digestion. Eking behaviour, another adaptation to starvation, is recruited to enhance food avoidance by prolonging the duration of meals. Food is cut up very small, eaten in tiny amounts and a meal may be prolonged to several hours as a result, with very little nutritional intake. Condiment abuse, found in non-eating disordered starving people, is common in patients with eating disorders trying to limit their nutritional intake. It to some extent satisfies the need to taste, and acts as a way to avoid intake of nutritional foods. Moreover, some patients use it to render food inedible:

### Patient F

*A patient with Anorexia Nervosa in a day hospital chose a plate of food with a reasonable nutritional content. She then covered the food with successive layers of tomato ketchup, brown sauce, black pepper and mayonnaise. She then pronounced it (reasonably) as inedible and left the table.*

Lastly, the biological urge to eat may be suppressed using appetite suppressant drugs, some prescribed (usually unscrupulously) but mostly obtained illegally, including amphetamine, MDMA and cocaine. The patient's struggle against her nutritional needs is bound to be a losing one, with a terrible psychological and physical price. Filling the stomach with non-nutrient matter has been tried by starving people throughout history, with little success, while laboratory studies of sham feeding rats whose oral intake is diverted by creating a hole between the stomach and the abdominal skin, so that food never gets past the stomach, have shown that taste stimulation alone does not produce satiety (Young *et al.*, 1974).

*Disposing of food*   This symptom is closely related to the degree to which food is eaten, either as a result of overwhelming nutritional need, as in binge-eating, or when family or health care workers insist on meals or other nutrition being taken, against the wishes of the patient. In the context of pressure from the family or from staff, food may be hidden or thrown away:

## Patient G

*A patient with SEED (Anorexia Nervosa bulimic subtype) was admitted to a general psychiatric ward where she stayed for several weeks, gaining very little weight. She was observed to take regular baths, and after her discharge, patients complained about a stench in the bathroom. On investigation, the bath panels were unscrewed to reveal a large cache of rotting food concealed behind the panels.*

Purging behaviour is a common way, in anorexia and bulimia nervosa, to dispose of food ingested either in binges or under coercion. Here again, a physiological change which may favour adaptation to starvation (delayed gastric emptying) is recruited to the service of food disposal, as patients are aware that they can wait for some time and still be able to vomit the majority of a meal, thanks to delayed gastric emptying which can hold the food in the stomach for up to several hours.

Laxative abuse is the other common way to dispose of food that has already been ingested. There is a sharp difference of opinion between doctors and patients about the efficacy of laxative abuse as a way of preventing absorption. The former point to the efficiency of the small intestine's absorptive power, and the lack of evidence for laxative-induced malabsorption, while patients say that they see chunks of undigested food in their stools. I suspect that the necessary research to settle this has yet to be done, because of the difficulty of interesting a grant giving body to fund a study and the reluctance of potential researchers to analyse large quantities of diarrhoeal stool in pursuit of an answer to the question! Laxative abuse does seem to clear the abdomen of bulk, and the feeling of emptiness, and of having a flat tummy is highly valued, as is the weight loss, which may be due to dehydration, occurring after a large dose of laxatives. A specific form of laxative abuse is reflected in the practice of using the anti-obesity drug Orlistat, which prevents fat absorption by blocking the fat breakdown enzyme, Lipase, in the gut, to lose weight in eating disorders. Sometimes the drug is prescribed by doctors, possibly inappropriately, but more commonly it is obtained via the Internet.

A group of patients dispose of nutrients by failing to treat a disease which causes malnutrition. One example is the case of a patient with diabetes mellitus who encourages the excretion of glucose in the urine by reducing or eliminating her insulin treatment. Another is provided by the patient with inflammatory bowel disease (e.g. Crohn's disease) who misses out her dose of steroids to encourage diarrhoea, or the patient with gluten enteropathy (Coeliac disease) who deliberately eats gluten to induce diarrhoea and malabsorption.

*Increasing energy consumption*   The most common way of increasing energy usage is by exercise which can be high intensity and relatively brief, as in training or running, or low intensity and prolonged, as in walking, which may go on for several hours per day. Obsessional symptoms have been noted to be associated with both eating disorders and starvation, and obsessive preoccupation with food may enhance survival when the search for something to eat must be the priority. However, in eating disorders (as in starvation) obsessionality extends beyond the realm of food, and is used to achieve energy wastage – e.g. through excessive housework. A few patients, mostly with medical connections, use thyroid hormone to enhance metabolism and thereby waste energy and lose weight. Apart from being dangerous to the heart, this practice is probably not very effective in its stated aim. It will perhaps become more widespread as the Internet is used to bypass medical monitoring of such medication.

## Eating disorders in patients with symptoms beyond nutrition and body image

### Patient B

*This 20-year-old woman, already mentioned in Chapter 1, was admitted to hospital under Section 3 of the Mental Health Act due to severe weight loss (to 35 kg, BMI 13.4). She had begun restricting her diet at the age of 13 as a result of 'bullying' by her older sister, and had received various forms of treatment for her eating disorder from child psychiatric and general adult services. Two years before admission, her sister had been involved in a serious road traffic accident and had suffered brain damage for which she was receiving rehabilitation. Apart from the 'bullying', there had been a history of illness in childhood with hospitalization for chest, bowel and orthopaedic problems. From 8 to 9$^{1}/_{2}$ years of age, she was on crutches following foot surgery. She was diagnosed as dyslexic and required remedial education due to this. After admission, she was found to be very depressed and to be experiencing critical auditory hallucinations. She gained weight with regular meals and began individual group and family therapy with her parents. The depression and hallucinations continued when she reached a healthy weight, and she repeatedly self-harmed with cigarette burns, scratching herself, banging her head and she took overdoses with clear*

**Table 2.1** Some of the symptoms of eating disorders are presented in terms of their relation to the requirements to survive and to have a thin body. Many of the symptoms in the third column will be seen to antagonize those in the fifth

| Nutritional area | Survival requirement | Symptom | Body image requirement | Symptom |
|---|---|---|---|---|
| Food consumption | Eating | Thinking, dreaming about food | Not eating | Body image distortion |
| | | Feeding others | | Guilt at adequate nutrition |
| | | Work in catering | | Enhanced satiety |
| | | Binge eating | | Eking behaviour |
| | | Non-nutritional eating | | Condiment abuse |
| | | | | Appetite suppressant drugs |
| Food conservation | Conservation | Eking behaviours (see text) | Disposal | Hiding food |
| | | Enhanced satiety | | Vomiting |
| | | Hoarding | | Laxative abuse |
| | | | | Medication omission |
| Energy conservation | Conservation | Social withdrawal | Wastage | Exercise |
| | | Reduced thyroid activity | | Obsessional cleaning |
| | | Hyposexuality | | Thyroid hormone abuse |
| | | Infertility | | |

*suicidal intent, in spite of escalating nursing observations, including 24 hour one-to-one nursing. She was given antidepressant and antipsychotic medication, but developed allergic liver reactions to several drugs. As her depression, psychosis and self-harm were all very severe and life-threatening she was given a course of electro-convulsive therapy, which resulted in a major improvement. She began to use individual and family therapy more effectively. During one session with her parents, she disclosed that the 'bullying' from her sister from the age of 12 (just before she began dietary restriction) had in fact been in the form of sadistic and humiliating sexual abuse which went on regularly until she was 17. It stopped when her sister was injured in the accident. The revelation caused extreme distress in the family, who had hitherto been unaware of the abuse. Soon after that session, Patient B developed a spasm in her right leg muscles. She had had regular spasms for a number of years, responding to passive stretching. This spasm was disabling and did not respond to any physical therapy. She was referred to a consultant anaesthetist who recommended epidural anaesthetic block. Following this procedure she became bed-bound, almost paralyzed from the waist down, and incontinent, and spent 6 months in a neurology unit requiring a urinary catheter and enemas for constipation, in part, due to chronic laxative abuse. Investigations showed no neurological explanation for her disability. Contact was maintained with the eating disorders staff who visited her regularly, and she expressed a wish to come back to the eating disorders unit. This could only be agreed if she was walking and continent, and over the next few weeks her condition improved to a point at which she was able to return. Treatment then concentrated on her psychological difficulties with continued individual and family therapy with the addition of Eye Movement Desensitization and Reprocessing (EMDR) (National Collaborating Centre for Mental Health, 2005) treatment. The reason for the latter was the recurrent terrifying images of abuse from which she suffered. During EMDR she was able to deal with many of the images, although at several times during therapy new and more disturbing images would appear, requiring further treatment. She was able to tolerate medication, and received antidepressant and antipsychotic drugs. She gradually improved and after a period as a day patient was able to be discharged, at a normal weight, continuing individual, family and EMDR therapy. Her discharge was 4 years after her original admission.*

*Commentary on patient B*   The number of diagnoses attracted by this patient were legion and included the following:

Anorexia Nervosa
Psychotic depression
Somatoform disorder
Post-traumatic stress disorder.

Her original eating disorder closely followed the onset of abuse from her sister, while the onset of severe somatoform disorder followed the revelation of the abuse during family therapy. The form of the somatic symptoms (spasm of her right leg) reflected similar symptoms during multiple previous episodes of spasm, all of which had been reversible within a few hours by physiotherapy. The subsequent deterioration with paralysis and incontinence occurred after an anaesthetic intervention and demonstrates the danger of such treatments in a predisposed patient. Her impressive ability to overcome her symptoms is demonstrated by her determination to get back from the neurology ward to a place where her psychological problems could be addressed, which meant giving up some of her somatic symptoms. The use of EMDR in PTSD is well documented (National Collaborating Centre for Mental Health, 2005) and in view of her flashbacks was clearly indicated in this patient's case. What of her psychotic symptoms? She described auditory hallucinations that were congruent with her severely depressed mood. Initially it was thought possible that these symptoms were related to malnutrition, and might improve with weight gain. This did not prove to be the case, and in view of the threat to her life, physical treatments including ECT were pursued. This treatment made essential psychological treatment possible. She first alluded to sexual abuse in her individual therapy, and a crisis came when she managed to discuss it in family therapy, in the absence of her sister. There followed a long period in which she did not see her sister, but subsequently she had called her, seen her and confronted her with what happened, although the sister, now brain damaged as a result of her accident, confesses no memory of the abuse. Patient B's self-harm reached a peak during weight gain, and occasioned escalation of nursing observations so that for a considerable time she was being observed constantly. Self-damaging behaviours, in common with all behaviours, do not occur in isolation from the social environment. It can be postulated that this patient was desperate to engage in close relationships with adults she perceived as being able to protect and nurture her. This may well underlie the apparently overprotective and over close relationships that many patients with eating disorders develop with their mothers. In a ward, patients rapidly get to learn that the more they exhibit self-damaging behaviour, the more observation they get. Some have confided that there can develop a competition in a unit for who is on the highest level of care. Getting onto a 'section', being nursed one-to-one, and even two-to-one, can all be seen (by a patient group) as desirable signs that someone is receiving higher levels of care, and that a patient lower down the hierarchy of control is somehow less 'loved' than someone higher up. This unfortunate process is most likely to occur in inpatient units with the most severely ill, compulsorily treated patients. In the case of Patient B, it is possible that some of her self-damaging behaviour was, indeed, related to this pursuit of controlling nurture. Given that serious incidents such as suicide or serious self-harm are usually followed by enquiries that criticize low levels of observation in someone known to be at risk for self-harm, it is difficult to see how inpatient units can always avoid this difficult outcome. Some units for patients with personality disorders (www.thecasselhospital.org) do not accept patients under compulsion and may discharge patients who self-harm, thereby limiting the process in their units, although the range of patients that can be treated is also limited as a result.

Patient B provides an example of a patient with severe and unstable eating disorder, who had several years of instability and hospital care before being able to continue her treatment and her life in the community.

### Patient H

*This 22-year-old was referred for admission after a 10-year history of Anorexia Nervosa. She had begun dieting after her first period at the age of 12, and at 14 reached a low weight (35 kg, BMI 12.8) although her GP was reported to have reassured the family that she would be OK. Bingeing and vomiting soon followed and remained a feature of her illness throughout. She was first treated at 17 in a general psychiatry unit near her home. This had only limited success, and at 19 she was referred for specialist treatment far from her home. She had several admissions during which she gained weight only to lose it after returning home. She had been tube-fed in a general medical ward several times, but always lost the weight rapidly when the tube was removed. She had spent most of the time from ages 17 to 20 in hospital, under Section 3 of the Mental Health Act. During her latest admission, she became unable to eat food that was presented, and she agreed to transfer to another unit. On admission she was very thin, BMI 11.3, and had muscle weakness, with difficulty getting up from squatting and sitting up from lying flat (the SUSS test; Robinson, 2006a). She felt very depressed and hopeless, and had frequent thoughts of self-harm and suicide. For several weeks she ate very little, but maintained her low weight, and required constant supervision to prevent her from committing suicide. In spite of the presence of a nurse, she managed a number of times to bang her head against the wall of her room. Later, when supervision was relaxed, she was found in a cupboard, trying to hang herself, which occasioned a further increase in supervision. However, by 5 months after admission, her weight had increased to 44 kg, without tube feeding and her mood was more stable, with less self-damaging behaviour, helped perhaps by the use of antipsychotic and antidepressant drugs. However, she continued to attempt to leave hospital, on one occasion making it to the airport so she could fly home. Her individual therapy became less food and weight focused, and her parents flew in for regular family sessions. Her weight stabilized at 44–45 kg (BMI 16.6–17), and it was clear that she was unable to increase her weight beyond this level without extreme distress. This low, but survivable weight was, therefore, accepted by the team as a maintenance weight and rehabilitation continued. She moved to the hospital hostel, and had a comprehensive rehabilitative programme including sessions during which she was helped to order food at restaurants and buy suitable clothes. A very supportive hostel was found near her home, and she obtained voluntary employment in her father's company. Contacts were made with the local community mental health team and the consultant in the Eating Disorders Team flew to the patient's hometown for a meeting. She was discharged from the Eating Disorders Service in December 2006, 5 years after her first referral.*

*Her early history gave little clue as to the origin of her eating disorder. She was the older of two sisters, and her weight loss and amenorrhoea had begun after having one menstrual period at the age of 12, when she went to the more academic school in the neighbourhood, while all her friends went to the less academic school. She moved schools to the latter at the age of 15 when her parents realized how unhappy she was. From the onset at 12, it was 2 years before she saw her general practitioner and a further 3 years before she was referred for local treatment and 2 more years when, at 19, she eventually entered specialist treatment. During these 5 years, her identity became firmly fixed as a thin girl, academically gifted, but unhappy and unassertive in every way apart from what she would eat. She frequently alluded to smacking by her father when she was a child, and this was admitted by the father to have occurred at times when her behaviour had become difficult. As a small child she would have prolonged tantrums during which she would throw herself to the floor and bang her head. There had been some birth asphyxia from which she was rapidly resuscitated, and no other reason was found for her childhood behavioural difficulties. Her relationship with her father improved markedly as her illness improved. Her relationship with her mother had always been extremely close and protective, and she found it difficult to be separate from her. Latterly, her mother had herself lost a substantial amount of weight, probably as a result of depression, particularly during the terminal illness of her own mother during her daughter's treatment in hospital. She reasonably argued that having a mother and a daughter with very serious illnesses was enough to lead anyone into depression.*

*Commentary on patient H* This young woman developed Anorexia Nervosa at the age of 12. There was a substantial delay before her condition was diagnosed and an appropriate referral made, and this delay may well have contributed to the severity of her illness. Unlike Patient B, no experience of major trauma was revealed during assessment or prolonged therapy, although her birth trauma may have affected her behaviour as a child, and there was at least some paternal smacking. She alludes to the difficulty of settling in to a school with none of her friends present, and it seems likely that she was less resilient than many children in that difficult circumstance and that this may have contributed to her eating disorder which began soon afterwards.

Diagnostically she fulfilled the criteria for Anorexia Nervosa, bulimic subtype and severe depression with frequent self-harm. It is of interest that there was a history of a form of self-harm (head banging) in childhood, and that formed a prominent part of her self-harming behaviour during treatment.

The long delay before treatment was even begun made that treatment particularly difficult. She had developed into a very shy 17-year-old, extremely dependent on her mother, with few friends and social skills. Her identity as a young woman with Anorexia Nervosa was entrenched and she knew no other. While this may have been feasible as a child and young adolescent, it unravelled when she entered the higher reaches of her school and looked towards university, perhaps boyfriends and separation from the family. During the first attempts at treatment, the aim was to help her get to a healthy weight, but her anorexic thinking and behaviour rapidly took control as soon she was released and within a few weeks she was back in a life-threatening state requiring immediate admission, usually under compulsion. This cycle characterized her life from 17 to 22 years. Experience in the most recent admission was similar, and intensive observation, compulsion and the possibility of tube feeding were all required initially. However, she gradually saw the possibility that she might have another sort of life, and that such a difference might be desirable. Hitherto, such a life meant giving up her special status as perpetual inpatient and trying to succeed in the outside world from which, like a long-term psychiatric inpatient from a 1950s mental hospital, she had become alienated. Acquiring the motivation to move from someone whose illness was always life-threatening, to someone who was still ill, but in a less acutely dangerous way, was a crucial step. In terms of complexity theory, it appeared that the formula of the strange attractor had been changed, so that the output was quite different. How does that occur? Perhaps the passage of time has an impact on someone who (like Alice in Wonderland) is aware that there is a doorway to a different life, sees the bottle labelled Drink Me, and comes to realize that the contents have a 'Best Before' date, so that if you wait 10 years, you may find the door has disappeared. Patients who ask 'When will I give up this obsession with weight loss?' are sometimes told 'When you find something more interesting to occupy your thoughts!' The processes of hospitalization and the various therapies and experiences to which the patient is exposed are so complex that it is almost impossible to determine what has been effective in a particular case. Similar approaches have such differing effects in different patients, some becoming able to relinquish the eating disorder, others remaining in its grip, that some change in the patient seems essential. The requirements of the therapeutic team are numerous. They have to be able to monitor all the changes in the patient's physiology, mental state and family and therapeutic environment, and respond to each change appropriately and consistently explaining each decision to the patient even though she may fiercely disagree with it. There has to be sufficient time at a sufficient level of stability for trusting relationships to build up with team members. The team has to be able to survive the fragmentation that can occur when one team member is singled out as the 'good mother' and another as the 'bad mother' (Petot and Trollope, 1991). Lastly, the team has to be able to let go and take some risks when the patient is ready. This can be quite difficult, not least because psychiatric systems became increasingly risk averse during the same period which saw a huge decrease in the availability of long-term psychiatric hospitalization. Teams, therefore, have to take risks knowing that they may not be supported by their managers (in the form of the inevitable enquiry which follows a serious incident) if things go wrong. The message is: 'Community care yes, sell the hospital for conversion to luxury flats – but make sure the patient and society are safe.'

As in Patient B, it has to be considered that some of the self-damaging behaviour expressed by Patient H might have been related to hospitalization itself. It is, indeed, quite likely that the inpatient setting, especially when one-to-one nursing is introduced, leads to escalating behavioural disturbance by the patient. She is usually feeling unsafe. She is gripped by a process that leads her to lose weight, with no lower target in sight, so she is out of control. Eating anything is experienced as the first step to massive obesity, and is equally out of control. The constant escalation of self-starvation, vomiting, self-harm, abscondion and many other behaviours could be seen as signs of the patient's determination to lose weight, and equally as signs of her terror at being out of control which can only be assuaged when the hospital, the Mental Health Act and the constantly supervising nurse (sometimes two or more) are all in place. Staff in this situation are in an unenviable dilemma, bearing in mind the pressures to keep everyone safe. An important role of the most senior person in the team, the lead clinician, is to take responsibility for risks that are inevitable if the patient is ever going to leave hospital.

This patient suffers from SEED. From the ages of 17 to 26 it was unstable, with frequent admissions following one after another. After prolonged in-patient care, she has settled in a supportive community hostel with full local psychiatric support, after a year's outpatient follow-up at the Eating Disorders Service, as recommended by NICE (National Collaborating Centre for Mental Health, 2004). After discharge (December 2005), she remained underweight with some fluctuations in weight but no need for further admission for the following 2 years. After the unstable phase of her illness passed, she was able to engage in rehabilitation. Using the headings of the Care Programme Approach, this consisted of the following:

1. *Medical care.* Regular outpatient consultations. Monitoring of medication (antidepressant, antipsychotic (olanzapine) and anti-anxiety (diazepam)) with reducing schedule for diazepam and olanzapine.
2. *Recognition of relapse.* Weight loss, depression, failure to engage in usual activities. Response: urgent psychiatric assessment.
3. *Psychological care.* Supportive sessions with her key worker at the hostel. Training in going out for a meal, buying clothes, socializing, budgeting, self-care while at eating disorders unit.
4. *Family care.* Support for parents from CMHT. Family therapy on request.
5. *Occupational and academic issues.* Voluntary job at father's firm. Advice on training courses and work experience.
6. *Social life.* Participation in groups at hostel. Advice on embarking on wider social life from key worker.
7. *Accommodation issues.* Hostel placement. Discussion of future options.
8. *Financial issues.* Help with obtaining state benefits. Budgeting help.

### Patient I

*This 40-year-old lady was referred after being found emaciated during a home visit she requested from her GP. She had developed problems with food and weight at the age of 11, had remained moderately underweight and then lost more weight in her 20s. She had abused laxatives in her teens, and developed chronic constipation and rectal prolapse as a result. In her family there had been violence between her parents, and between her and her younger sister, and their mother had attempted suicide. All her relatives lived abroad. Apart from the emaciation (BMI 12.7), her flat was in a serious state of disarray with papers piled up to a height of around 3 feet all over the living room. She explained that she had great difficulty making decisions, and had never been able to throw anything away. Over the previous 5 years, she had had a pattern of consulting many different doctors for a wide variety of medical complaints, including epilepsy, would receive treatment from several doctors at the same time, who were not aware of the other consultations, and was taking 27 different forms of medication. Over a 3-year period, she had been registered with five different GPs. She had never seen a psychiatrist.*

*Commentary on patient I*   This patient presents an extremely complex array of problems. She had suffered from an eating disorder since the age of 11, and presented with severe physical deterioration as a result of long-term self-neglect. She also had a long list of medical problems including epilepsy and constipation arising from damage to her colon due to laxative abuse, part of her eating disorder. Her home, with its mountains of paper, through which she had created Himalayan-style pathways to key locations such as bed and toilet, was eloquent testimony to her obsessive compulsive disorder. Lastly, her pattern of repeated multiple consultations to medical practitioners (but notably excluding a psychiatrist until the present referral, which was initiated by her General Practitioner) was evidence of three aspects of her difficulties. (1) She did have a lot of physical complaints. (2) Her physical state did not always reflect her reported symptoms. For example, she would report having several fits during a conversation in which her flow of speech and cognitive state were unimpaired. (3) She was frequently dissatisfied with her medical advisors and went through them at a very rapid rate. These are all characteristics of somatization disorder (DSM IV, American Psychiatric Association, 1994), one of the psychiatric disorders that is most difficult to manage due to the pattern of multiple consultations.

Obsessive compulsive disorder is commonly associated with eating disorders, especially Anorexia Nervosa. The association may be via a number of mechanisms (Hsu, Kaye and Weltzin, 1993; Thornton and Russell, 1997). There is often a previous history of obsessive compulsive traits and sometimes a family history of OCD, or OC traits, suggesting a genetic component. Secondly, malnutrition can be associated with obsessive compulsive symptoms. This was found in the classic Minnesota study (Keys *et al.*, 1950) in which previously healthy males were subjected to dietary deprivation and, in addition to depression and some bulimic symptoms, several of the participants developed obsessive compulsive symptoms, often related to food. Starvation-induced preoccupation with food is well described in Solzhenitsyn's 'One day in the life of Ivan Denisovich':

*Now for that slice of sausage. Into the mouth. Getting your teeth into it. Your teeth. The meaty taste. And the meaty juice, the real stuff. Down it goes, into your belly. Gone.*

A further route to obsessional symptoms is through depression, which occurs in many underweight patients with Anorexia Nervosa. The aetiology of depression in eating disorders is complex and nutritional, genetic and situational factors probably all play a part. A proportion of depressed patients with Anorexia Nervosa will also suffer from obsessive compulsive symptoms. Lastly, compulsive behaviour can form part of the patient's anorexic routine, contributing to weight loss and a sense of control.

### Patient J

*A woman of 38 had suffered from Anorexia Nervosa since her teens, with a persistent BMI of 15. She had very low self-esteem, and a powerful drive for thinness. Her obsessional rituals included 5 hours of housework per day. Keeping her house clean gave her a feeling of achievement and burnt off a significant proportion of the calories she ingested during the day. Her meals also had obsessional characteristics. She would eat exactly similar food at the same time each day. Any change in her routine, such as missing her usual start time, led her to abandon a meal. The housework, the constancy of food ingested and the insistence on uniformity are all characteristics of obsessive compulsive disorder but coincidentally keep weight down by burning calories, controlling the calorie content of meals and encouraging meals to be missed at times.*

### Patient K

*This 27-year-old woman was referred because of increasing restriction, increasing preoccupation with food and weight, occasional bingeing and abuse of diet pills. She had had difficulties with eating since the age of 12 when although she had a normal weight she began to diet. At 14 she began bingeing and vomiting, and subsequently lost weight and developed amenorrhoea. Her bulimia did not lead to medical referral but at 18 when her BMI was 14.7 she was admitted to a private unit, the first of 8 such admissions. Each admission consisted of*

*4 weeks, funded by insurance, followed by discharge after which she would drop out of follow-up. The latest admission was for a 12 step programme aimed at alcohol dependence during which she was told that she was intolerant of white flour and sugar and encouraged to exclude them, which led to an increase in dietary restriction and bulimia. Her insurance company had, after 8 years funding, deemed her condition chronic and refused any further funding.*

*At 16 she began using alcohol to excess and street drugs including cocaine, ecstasy and LSD. She described intense and frequent mood swings from very depressed with suicidal ideation, to hypomanic, with overspending and euphoria, insomnia and irritability. She wondered if she suffered from bipolar disorder, but assessment was complicated by her use of drugs and alcohol. She also gave a history of self-harm, with a number of drug overdoses while she was low, and cutting her arms superficially.*

*She was born into a middle-income family near to London the first of 3 daughters, with twins born 2 years after her. Her father often worked away, and her mother was always nervous and on edge. At 5 she was investigated for urinary retention but no cause found. She has wondered whether she was abused, but has no specific memories. She was the class clown at a private boarding school, and found concentration hard. She was never assessed for ADHD and after leaving school at 16, when drugs, alcohol and bulimia began, she was unable to hold down a job or have a relationship longer than a few weeks. She described feelings of emptiness and boredom. During treatment, she was unable to commit to long-term therapy and was a frequent attender at Accident and Emergency because of overdoses, alcohol toxicity or suicidal thoughts.*

*Commentary on patient K* This history is one of a patient with borderline personality disorder (see Table 2.2 for diagnostic criteria). It will be noted that an eating disorder symptom (binge eating) is one of the features that may be present. No other eating disorder symptoms are listed, however, so the overlap between eating disorders and BPD is confined to binge eating, other symptoms forming part of the wide spectrum of co-morbidity that can accompany eating disorders. The concept of a constellation of problems such that criteria for both ED and BPD are fulfilled has been around for some time. Lacey (Lacey and Evans, 1986) coined the term multi-impulsive bulimia (see Table 2.3 for suggested criteria), and developed inpatient care, which appears to be effective in motivated patients (Lacey and Read, 1993). Because of their multiple problems, it seems unlikely that one community

**Table 2.2** Diagnostic criteria for borderline personality disorder

---

A pervasive pattern of instability of interpersonal relationships, self-image, and
affects, and marked impulsivity beginning by early adulthood and present
in a variety of contexts, as indicated by five (or more) of the following:

1. Frantic efforts to avoid real or imagined abandonment.
2. A pattern of unstable and intense interpersonal relationships characterized
   by alternating between extremes of idealization and devaluation.
3. Identity disturbance: markedly and persistently unstable self-image or
   sense of self.
4. Impulsivity in at least two areas that are potentially self-damaging (e.g.
   spending, sex, substance abuse, reckless driving, binge eating).
5. Recurrent suicidal behaviour, gestures, or threats or self-mutilating
   behaviour.
6. Affective instability due to a marked reactivity of mood (e.g. intense
   episodic dysphoria, irritability or anxiety usually lasting a few hours and
   only rarely more than a few days).
7. Chronic feelings of emptiness.
8. Inappropriate, intense anger or difficulty controlling anger (e.g. frequent
   displays of temper, constant anger, recurrent physical fights).
9. Transient, stress-related paranoid ideation or severe dissociative symptoms.

---

service could provide for all of their needs. The minimum list of necessary
services would be:

1. Psychological therapies to address the underlying borderline personality disorder.
2. Eating disorder services to address eating and weight problems.
3. Drug and alcohol services.
4. Emergency and crisis services.

Splitting up the patient's treatment runs  the risk of therapists being
divided into good and bad, with the result that the treatment becomes
fragmented and ineffective. Ideally, all such services would be available in
the same team who would meet together regularly (including the patient)
and all subscribe to a single treatment plan. There is some justification for
sequencing the management of different problem areas. The reason for this
is that some behaviours inhibit treatment for others. Thus, major alcohol
or other drug abuse could compromise cognitive behavioural treatment for

**Table 2.3** Diagnostic criteria for multi-impulsive bulimia as defined by Lacey and Evans (1986)

1. Bulimia is associated with one or more of the following:
   Gross alcohol abuse
   'Street drug' abuse
   Multiple overdoses
   Repeated self-damage
   Sexual disinhibition
   Shoplifting
2. Each behaviour is associated with a similar sense of being out of control.
3. Each of these patterns of behaviour may fluctuate, and they are interchangeable and impulsive.
4. The patient's affects are of depression and intense anger, which are declared when the behaviours are controlled.

bulimia nervosa, while repeated self-harm can interfere with treatment for other problems because of the urgent requirement for medical care. Some patients can deal with their problems in sequence, so that they might attend a substance misuse service to get their use of drugs down to a manageable level. The patient could then attend individual or group therapy for bulimia nervosa or Anorexia Nervosa, while keeping the substance misuse under control. Approaches to self-harm vary. Dialectical Behaviour Therapy (DBT) (Linehan, 1993) and Mentalization Based Therapy (MBT) (Bateman and Fonagy, 2004) have both been shown to reduce the level of self-harm behaviours in people with the diagnosis of borderline personality disorder, and either could be used in a programme. A third approach is to use inpatient care (Lacey and Read, 1993) in which motivated patients are admitted to hospital for intensive individual and group therapy.

Outpatient care for a patient with a combination of a longstanding eating disorder and a borderline personality disorder could run along the following lines:

*Stage 1: address dangerous behaviours.* These behaviours would include consumption of potentially toxic levels of alcohol or other drugs, overdoses, life-threatening cutting, maintenance of a very low body weight and frequent bulimic episodes with electrolyte imbalance. Treatment of the eating disorder behaviours is thereby combined with management of other potentially hazardous symptoms.

*Stage 2: address residual symptoms that interfere with effective psychotherapy.* Patients at this stage would still have symptoms in a number of areas, including eating disorder, substance misuse and self-harm, but none is life-threatening.

*Stage 3: address underlying psychological difficulties.* Self-damaging behaviours are at a level at which psychotherapy such as DBT or MBT could safely be pursued.

The stages are not mutually exclusive. However if, for example, a patient is at stage 3, in psychotherapy, and she begins using heroin, turning up intoxicated for therapy sessions, then it would be appropriate to exclude her from that session and readmit her to therapy when she was not intoxicated. Moreover, if a patient in therapy loses weight, it could first be discussed in therapy, but if it continues and threatens to undermine psychotherapy, sessions may need to be redirected towards weight restoration until an agreed BMI has been reached. In this way, weight loss is treated in the same fashion as intoxication or self-harm, being addressed until the patient is safe at which time psychotherapy can resume.

## Summary

SEED may be characterized exclusively or mainly by symptoms referable to nutrition and body image, is described in the first part of this chapter. However, the eating disorder may only be a part of a much more widespread and pervasive disorder with many and varied symptoms, as described in the second part. Assessment and treatment needs to reflect the complexities found in both of these types of SEED and treatment teams may need to address problems in many different areas of psychiatry and general medicine.

# 3

# Medical Aspects of SEED

Long-term eating disorders present a number of processes of interest to the physician. Patients who continue to have severe symptoms for many years may be constantly at risk of a serious, acute medical problem. They live on the edge, and may gain some comfort, or even a thrill, from the knowledge that they are continuing to survive against the prognostications of the experts. Running alongside these constant risks, are gradually increasing medical problems that may only come to fruition later in life. These two classes of problem will be looked at separately, because they demand distinct approaches to assessment and treatment.

## Life on the Edge

Patients with long-term eating disorders sometimes live with physical states that seem incompatible with life: a BMI of 9.5, a potassium level of 1.9 mmol/l or a sodium level of 120 mmol/l. The fact that they do survive, is testament to the body's capacity to adjust to a changing internal milieu, and 'get used' to 'abnormal' states. The physician responsible for the medical care of a patient in this situation, whether a general practitioner, psychiatrist or nutrition physician, needs to appreciate that such lab or clinical findings are often not a reason to call an ambulance and begin resuscitation, as it might be in someone with a 6 month illness. In fact, rapid correction of such abnormalities can be extremely dangerous, and the experience of treating severe undernutrition teaches us that gradual correction,

*Severe and Enduring Eating Disorder*   Paul Robinson
© 2009 John Wiley & Sons, Ltd

or no change at all, may be much safer (Payne-James *et al.*, 2008). However, a patient with a BMI of 9.5 is nearer to physical collapse than someone in the normal weight range, and the clinical challenge is to monitor physical state frequently enough to identify dangerous processes, and to assess a wide enough variety of physiological measures, so that a life-threatening change is detected.

A case history will first be presented and then discussed in the light of the risks the patient was running.

### Patient L

*This young woman was referred at the age of 16 with amenorrhoea and weight loss since the age of 15 with a BMI of 14.8. She is the older of two children, with a brother some 5 years her junior. Her mother had suffered from severe inflammatory bowel disease for some years, and had frequently been ill with several hospitalizations. Patient L had become close to her father, who shared his problems with her from an early age. She was treated initially as an outpatient with individual and family therapy, failed to improve and was admitted to hospital where she gained weight, and her periods returned briefly. However, she then maintained her weight just below normal continuing outpatient therapy until, at 18, she went to a tropical country where she began to have abdominal pains and diarrhoea. Tests for infection were negative. She discontinued eating disorders care and saw a gastroenterologist. She also consulted a nutritionist who placed her on a no sugar, no wheat, no dairy diet. Over the following year, her weight fell to a BMI of 15.5. When she was 36 kg (BMI 13.8) the gastroenterologist referred her back urgently to eating disorders services, and she resumed outpatient treatment and began to put on weight. When it reached 42.5 kg (BMI 16) she again changed to the gastroenterology clinic and lost still more weight, refusing offers of outpatient follow-up. On referral back she had lost more weight, became very ill and was admitted to a coronary care unit hypothermic, with ECG abnormalities, at the age of 23. After resuscitation and weight gain in hospital, she lost weight again in outpatients and for the last 2 years her BMI has remained between 11.5 and 12.5. Her IBS symptoms have continued and she has stopped eating food altogether, surviving on a powdered elemental diet bought via the Internet, although she is not convinced that the diet helps her symptoms. She has a continued interest in writing and she is substantially gifted as a playwright, but her education has been constantly interrupted by her eating disorder and its treatment.*

## Commentary on Patient L

This sad story of the development of SEED in a young woman contains many lessons. The development of the illness at the age of 15 is hard to explain fully. She was a popular and gifted young woman, and the main problems were at home, where her mother had frequently been very ill, sometimes lying bleeding on the floor. Patient L felt responsible for the welfare of the family, as did her little brother, and she developed a very close relationship with her father.

Although a story could be constructed from this and other information, it does not really explain the disorder. The patient herself described how she never felt as she was growing up that her own needs were ever anyone's priority until she was so ill that it was proposed to place her on a Section of the Mental Health Act, when both her father and mother paid her exclusive attention. She is careful to avoid blaming her parents, and attributes her disorder to the major problems occurring in the family throughout her growing up. Her illness was of moderate severity until she visited a tropical country after which she developed symptoms of bowel disturbance which have had such a powerful effect on her treatment. She may have had a gut infection, such as Giardia, but none was ever isolated. The diagnosis of IBS led her to turn to gastroenterology, for help. Her consultation with a nutritionist led to a disastrous downturn in her eating disorder. Her avoidance of some of the most essential nutrients was medically sanctioned and she lost weight rapidly. The most dangerous aspect of this was that her eating disorder treatment was suspended and the patient refused to attend for appointments. Only when she had lost a massive amount of weight was she referred back (in something of a panic) by the gastroenterologist. Since that time all gastroenterology consultations have been either jointly with the eating disorders team, or explicitly sanctioned by them. Such joint working is more feasible in the National Health Service, in which the GP has some more control of the referral process, than in private practice, in which many doctors see patients without the involvement of the GP, or of other relevant practitioners who have been involved in the patient's care.

## Medical Monitoring of a Patient with SEED

In a patient suffering from Anorexia Nervosa of long duration, there are a number of domains within the medical sphere that need to be addressed.

**Table 3.1** Physical measures used to monitor risk

| Function | Measure | Critical levels |
| --- | --- | --- |
| Body weight | BMI | <14 |
| Electrolytes | Na | <130 mmol/l |
| | K | <3 mmol/l |
| Liver function tests | Transaminase levels | Increasing |
| Muscle strength | SUSS test | Decreasing |
| | CK | Increasing |
| Cardiac function | ECG | Any serious change |
| | CK-MB | >5% total CK |

Firstly, the patient may be in such a poor physical condition that frequent monitoring is necessary to keep her alive. Secondly, continuing physical symptoms, while not life-threatening, may impair functioning and lastly, long-term consequences of symptoms of the eating disorder may lead to other disabilities.

## What to measure (Table 3.1)

The main life-threatening changes in physiology that accompany eating disorders involve weight loss, electrolyte disturbances and cardiac abnormalities. Self-harm is an additional hazard usually linked to a psychiatric diagnosis. They are not substantially different in patients with SEED to those with more acute forms of eating disorder, but as mortality increases with length of illness, their relevance and danger become more important with time. Moreover, a team caring for a seriously ill patient for many years may become exhausted by the need for constant vigilance, and the collective eye can be taken off the ball, leading to potentially serious consequences.

The most important measures to keep under review are electrolytes, liver function tests, muscle function and the electrocardiograph.

*Electrolyte disturbances.* Each electrolyte is associated with a range of potentially dangerous symptoms.

*Sodium (Na).* This is sometimes abnormal in patients with eating disorders. Elevation of sodium can be due to dehydration, but the most common problem encountered is low sodium levels (less than 135 mmol/l). This is usually due to excessive consumption of water and, if extreme, can lead to convulsions.

### Patient M

*A 22-year-old woman with a history of anorexia and bulimia nervosa for 4 years was being treated as an outpatient. She was underweight, but not life-threateningly, and had a BMI of around 16. Her weight was rising gradually at about 1 kg per month with outpatient treatment and her family and the therapeutic team were not too concerned. On her way to therapy, one day, she had an epileptic fit and was found to have a sodium of 119 mmol/l (normal range 135 to 145). She was unconscious for 2 days, then confused for a further 2 days. MRI brain scan was normal and her sodium returned to normal. She was weighed on Day 5 and found to be 9.5 kg higher than her preadmission weight suggesting that she was waterloading 9.5 l (over 2 gallons) prior to weighing. She confided later that she had stood in the shower with the rose (the shower head) in her mouth in order to waterload.*

*Potassium.* Low potassium is very common in patients with eating disorders. It mostly occurs in patients who vomit, or abuse laxatives or diuretics. In the latter two cases, loss of potassium in urine or faeces probably contributes to hypokalaemia. In patients who vomit, those with bulimia nervosa and purging disorder, the cause is less direct. Loss of stomach acid during vomiting causes alkalosis, that is, the blood becomes alkaline. The body reacts to this unacceptable state by retaining acid in the kidney. However, it has to exchange the acid for something and that turns out to be potassium. The resulting loss of potassium does not show up in the blood for a time, because most potassium is inside cells. However, the stores are eventually depleted, and blood potassium declines. When that occurs, peripheral nerves become more excitable because under alkaline conditions calcium is encouraged back onto its carrier protein so less is available in solution, leading to changes in nerve function (e.g. tingling fingers) similar to those seen in low calcium states.

### Patient N

*A young woman was seen for an initial assessment. She was moderately underweight (BMI 17) and admitted to vomiting 3 times a week to control her weight. She was sent for a routine blood test and the blood-taker called to say that the patient's hand had gone into spasm soon after the tourniquet was applied. She was asked to wait for the results of the test and when the potassium came back at 1.6 mmol/l, a potentially fatal level, she was admitted to hospital for potassium replacement and cardiac monitoring.*

The spasm was due to reduced free calcium in the plasma. A medical monitoring policy must include both electrolyte measurement and a guide on what to do when the results are abnormal. Here is a policy on management of hypokalaemia in a community setting:

K 2.5–3.5.

Weekly monitoring.

ECG monitoring (look for U waves, ST and T changes and prolonged QTc (over 500 ms)).

Prescription of potassium supplements if vomiting or other purging behaviour persists. (Sando K$^®$ contains 12 mmol K$^+$. Use 2 to 8 tablets per day, depending on purging symptoms, potassium level and response to treatment.)

K 2–2.5.

Patient to stay in the unit or surgery for the day and take 72 mmol of KCl (6 tablets over the day).

Remeasure K level in the evening. If >2.5 mmol/l go home with supply of KCl. If <2.5 mmol/l request medical opinion for possible medical admission.

*Urea level.* Urea is the waste product of excess protein. It is made in the liver, and both reduced and raised levels have significance in eating disorders.

A low urea level usually means that an inadequate amount of dietary protein is being taken in. It is a useful confirmation that the patient is restricting her food intake if one is needed.

A high level has two common causes. One is inadequate water intake leading to reduced blood flow through the kidney and, hence an impairment in the kidney's capacity to pass urea from the blood into the urine. This is usually reversible with an increase in water intake. However, some patients with Anorexia Nervosa value the weight loss that accompanies dehydration and severely limit their fluid intake, risking the second cause of a raised urea, kidney failure.

### Patient O

*A young woman of 18 contacted the author by email writing: 'Perhaps something can help.' She had received treatment in the past for Anorexia Nervosa, but after some unsuccessful therapy she refused to continue and stayed in her room using the Internet to communicate with other people. Her intake consisted of one small vegetable pie and half a glass of water each day, and she had pursued this diet for over a year. She complained of thirst and had signs of dehydration.*

Her BMI was 11.2 and blood tests showed a grossly raised urea and creatinine with metabolic acidosis. She was admitted to hospital and was judged too frail for dialysis. She died within 12 hours of admission. The image that remains of her huge eyes and wasted frame still haunts. During her final hours she kept turning off her glucose drip because it had 'too many calories'.

This patient had severely restricted both her food and water as a result of her profound body image distortion. At presentation, she was already in terminal kidney failure. Her poignant email reflected her realization that she had gone too far, and wished to be rescued. Her high urea level was due to dehydration, but her kidneys had been irreparably damaged and so her creatinine rose. Creatinine comes from muscle and is usually low in Anorexia Nervosa due to low muscle mass. When it rises it suggests that kidney damage has occurred.

*Other electrolytes.* Chloride and bicarbonate may change in eating disorders, mostly as a result of vomiting or diarrhoea, but they generally follow other electrolytes, and do not provide much extra information. Magnesium can fall, especially in laxative abusing patients, and is often accompanied by low calcium. Low magnesium can interfere with recovery from low potassium, so both need to be addressed. Phosphate, as well as potassium, can fall precipitately when a patient is refed after a long fast. This is the *Refeeding Syndrome*, and must be anticipated in emaciated patients admitted to either medical or psychiatric inpatient care (Hearing, 2004). The syndrome can occur outside hospital:

### Patient P

*This patient in her 30s with a history of anorexia and bulimia nervosa since her teens, complicated by self-harm by cutting and head banging, and, previously, regular exsanguination, came to a care planning meeting having lost 4 kg in the previous 3 weeks. Her BMI was 13.2 and she was told that she would need to gain some weight in order to avoid hospital admission. She was warned against rapid refeeding and asked to increase her intake slowly. Arrangements were made for her to have blood tests for electrolytes and an ECG the following morning, a Thursday. At 5 p.m. on Thursday, the results of blood tests were obtained:*

*Potassium 2.0 mmol/l (NR 3.5–5)*
*Phosphate 0.39 mmol/l (NR 0.87–1.45)*

*An emergency GP visited her and persuaded her to attend Accident and Emergency that evening. She was admitted to hospital where refeeding syndrome was confirmed.*

*She admitted to having binged after leaving the meeting on Wednesday evening.*

*Liver function tests*   The liver function tests include pigments (bilirubin) and enzymes, including alkaline phosphatase and transaminases (AST and ALT). It is the latter, the transaminases, which commonly rise in eating disorders. Why this should happen is uncertain, but it does appear to be a significant indicator of severe malnutrition and a sign that a patient is heading towards hospital admission. Other causes of abnormal liver function need to be ruled out, the most common being alcohol abuse which does complicate Anorexia Nervosa if the patient can overcome her disinclination to take in so calorific a substance as alcohol.

*Muscle function*   Monitoring muscle function provides a simple and useful measure of nutritional status, and should always form part of the physical assessment of a patient at risk because of low BMI in Anorexia Nervosa. It is usefully quantified although the accepted method for assessing muscle power in neurology, the MRC scale is not helpful because it is too insensitive, so that patients score highly until they are extremely unwell. We have developed a scale, the SUSS test, which appears to be useful in these patients. The acronym stands for Sit Up Squat Stand.

The patient is asked to lie down flat on the floor, cleared of debris, and sit up without, if possible using her hands. In the second part, she is asked to squat and stand up straight. Scoring is the same for each part of the test on a 4-point scale as follows:

1. Unable to do the test at all.
2. Able to do the test, only by using hands or elbows to help.
3. Able to do the test, but with obvious difficulty.
4. Able to do the test with no difficulty.

This simple clinical test will identify muscle weakness as it occurs in patients with Anorexia Nervosa losing weight, and usually becomes abnormal as BMI falls below 14. It is useful when patients are suspected of attempting to falsify their weight by water loading or other means (see Robinson, 2006a). In the case described above (Patient M), there was evidence suggesting that the quantity of water consumed before weighing may have been nearly 10 l, a truly remarkable finding. In that case, the deception was discovered when the patient suffered a hyponatraemic fit. It is unlikely that the SUSS test would have helped, because at her BMI of around 16, her muscle power would most probably have been normal.

*Creatine kinase (CK) levels.* This enzyme is found in muscle, both in skeletal muscle and the heart. It is most commonly useful in two conditions, heart attack, in which damage to the heart is reflected in a raised CK, and muscle diseases such as polymyositis.

There are two forms of CK, one found mostly in skeletal muscle and the other (CK-MB) found more in the heart. In Anorexia Nervosa a raised CK, like high liver enzymes, usually means severe malnutrition, and is seen at BMIs under 14. The proportion of CK-MB in such patients is higher than the 5% usually considered normal, and this could mean that cardiac damage is occurring indicating the need for an ECG. However, a high CK-MB percentage could also be explained by the fact that in athletes (and some of our patients train hard!) the proportion of CK-MB in skeletal muscle rises, so a raised blood level in Anorexia Nervosa might not be cardiac. This leads on to the other major variable influencing CK levels, exercise. Patients who overexercise may have a transiently raised CK, which returns to normal after the end of the exercise.

Our experience is that an exercise-induced rise in CK is most likely in someone already underweight, with a raised CK level, which rises further (sometimes to very high levels) and then falls to a lower level after the exercise ends (or when it is prevented by inpatient nursing observations).

*Cardiac function*   CK-MB has already been mentioned, and at present the significance of a raised CK-MB percentage is uncertain. Electrocardiographs are, however, frequently abnormal in eating disorders and an ECG should form part of the initial evaluation in all patients in whom low weight or electrolyte abnormalities contribute to the clinical picture. Abnormalities in the ECG can be classified as those associated with electrolyte disturbances and the rest.

1. *ECG abnormalities associated with electrolyte disturbance.* As indicated above, the most common dangerous electrolyte problem is hypokalaemia, and this usually occurs in patients who vomit or abuse laxatives or diuretics. ECG anomalies include U waves, inverted T waves and prolonged corrected QT interval (QTc). Arrhythmias, including ventricular extrasystoles, are also observed. The level below which ECG anomalies occur varies between individuals. Potassium of 1.9 mmol/l has been asymptomatic in one male patient with bulimia nervosa, while a female patient with Anorexia Nervosa developed ventricular tachycardia at a K of 2.3 mmol/l. It is a good idea to indicate clearly on the patient record that a particular problem occurred at a specified potassium level.

2. *ECG changes not apparently associated with electrolyte imbalance.* Patients who lose weight frequently have ECG changes with no observed electrolyte disturbance. The latter cannot always be ruled out, because all possible electrolytes and micronutrients may not have been measured, the usual suspects being magnesium, calcium and thiamine. However, on present evidence it seems very likely that low weight is associated with ECG anomalies. The usual appearance is commonly that associated with ischaemia, namely inversion of the T wave and elevation or depression of the ST segment. It is unlikely that coronary blood flow is reduced, as it is in angina, and the most plausible explanation is that myocardial metabolism is compromised due to loss of cardiac muscle and depletion of energy (i.e. glycogen) stores in the heart. Like many issues in the field of eating disorders (see Chapter 9), this remains to be investigated.

*How frequent?*   Given that an abnormality in a potentially critical physiological measure has been identified, how frequently should it be monitored? The answer depends on two main characteristics: the nature of the change and how long it has been at this level. Some changes need urgent action whenever they are detected, a serious cardiac arrhythmia, an acute abdominal problem such as gastric dilatation or volvulus (twisting) of the colon. These types of change are uncommon, however. Most changes, such as low BMI, low sodium and even low potassium, if they develop slowly, and persist for months or years, may not present a major short-term risk. This means that the patient can remain an outpatient or day patient without urgent hospital admission. The physician has to be convinced that the change is stable and long-term, however. Even then, monitoring may well be frequent (once or twice weekly, sometimes daily) at first, before it is clear that the patient has adapted to the abnormal result, and that urgent correction is not advisable. In practice, with time the team members become increasingly reassured that a low BMI is stable and long term, so that frequency of observations can be decreased. It is also the case, however, that someone with very abnormal results has less reserve than a less compromised patient, and it is advisable to continue weekly monitoring in someone with very abnormal results (e.g. a BMI of <14, a potassium <3 mmol/l or sodium <130 mmol/l).

### Physical problems related to long duration of symptoms

A number of physiological changes develop over time in patients with SEED. Some are related to maintaining a low body weight over a prolonged period, and some to purging behaviours associated with bulimia. Symptoms referable to these changes should be sought regularly, and appropriate investigations arranged should symptoms occur. Many physicians order routine investigations (such as bone mineral density measures) at intervals, whether or not symptoms occur.

*Osteoporosis*   It has been known for some time that patients with Anorexia Nervosa were at higher than average risk for osteoporosis. The proposed causes are several, including poor calcium and vitamin D intake, low oestrogen levels, raised cortisol levels and low weight. The latter theory is also expressed as 'semi-weightlessness'. It is well known that space travel can result in reduction in bone density due to the lack of stress on the skeleton during weightlessness (Keller, Strauss and Szpalski, 1992). Similar changes may occur in Anorexia Nervosa as a result of reduced weight. Moreover, in an interesting study (Galusca *et al.*, 2008) women with constitutionally low BMI (not amenorrhoeic or anorexic) were compared with AN patients with similar BMI. The constitutionally thin group had low bone density.

Bone mineral density is estimated using a scanner which passes a beam of x-rays through the body in selected places and, instead of producing a film for inspection, the machine (a DEXA scanner) produces a series of values. Because machines have not usually been standardized for examination of children, full results are available only for adults of over 18 years. The absolute values for bone density are not that useful without normal population data, and the most helpful figures to look for are the T-scores.

These are statistics (standard deviations) that give an indication of how far the patient's bone density at a particular site (usually hip or spine) deviates from the age-matched control population. The WHO has helpfully given a classification system for these results: Taking the total T-score for the spine, and for the hip, the following ranges apply:

T-score −1 to −2.5: osteopaenia
T-score under −2.5 (i.e. more negative, e.g. −3.5): osteoporosis.

A score in either range increases the chance of fractures after relatively minor trauma such as falls and can lead to increased disability from a fractured radius (such as Colles fracture of the wrist from falling on an outstretched arm), hip or spine. The latter leads to loss of height and some optimistic patients, having recalculated their BMI level after a loss of height, enquire whether they have now recovered from their Anorexia Nervosa as their BMI is now normal. It is evident that in calculating BMI the maximum adult height should be used, even though shortening of stature due to osteoporosis-induced crush fractures of the vertebrae may have occurred.

Treatment of osteoporosis or osteopaenia due to Anorexia Nervosa is simple in principle but often extremely difficult to achieve in practice. It had been shown clearly that weight gain helps increase bone density and that advice is the only evidence-based treatment available at present. Other interventions, which could potentially be effective, include calcium and vitamin D, oestrogen and biphosphonates.

*Calcium and Vitamin D*   These are essential for bone health, although lack of them is more likely to be associated with rickets (in children) and osteomalacia (in adults) than osteoporosis. In the low dairy and fat diet of someone with Anorexia Nervosa, both are likely to be deficient (Affenito *et al.*, 2002). However, evidence of the efficacy of calcium and vitamin D in ameliorating osteoporosis in Anorexia Nervosa is lacking. A therapeutic dose is unlikely to do harm although some patients baulk at the size of the tablets, and until the question of efficacy is answered this (Calcium and Vitamin D) is not unreasonable treatment. The other treatments are more controversial, since none has been found to ameliorate osteoporosis in Anorexia Nervosa, and all have, at least theoretical side effects. Oestrogens are commonly given, either as the oral contraceptive or as Hormone Replacement Therapy. Administration of these hormones have proven risks including thrombosis, uterine, ovarian and breast cancer (Gottlieb, 2001), and these albeit small risks must be weighed against the unproven benefit of oestrogen treatment of osteoporosis in Anorexia Nervosa in which the evidence is quite different from that in postmenopausal osteoporosis in which HRT has established benefit, although remains controversial (Stevenson, 2005). Biphosphonates are drugs used to encourage bone formation (Solomon, 2002) and are widely used in osteoporosis. The drug manufacturers limit the drugs to men and to postmenopausal women. The reason for this is that the drugs have a very long half-life in the body, some as long as 10 years, because of their binding to bone, and there is a theoretical risk that drug bound in bone could be transmitted to a foetus, hence the restriction to non-childbearing individuals. A further group who could be considered are those with very long-term SEED who are unlikely ever to recover and become pregnant. It is a very confident clinician, indeed, who can make such a prediction with certainty, though perhaps not a wise one. A patient in this situation who makes a fully informed decision can be offered biphosphonates, or one of the other bone-enhancing drugs such as Strontium. Evidence for efficacy is very sparse in the group of patients with Anorexia Nervosa so results may be disappointing. A further type of treatment using insulin-like growth factor may have a beneficial effect (National Collaborating Centre for Mental Health, 2005) but has not yet been used much in practice. Lastly, exercise which seems to have some role in the treatment of postmenopausal osteoporosis (Zehnacker and Bemis-Dougherty, 2007) has not been formally evaluated in Anorexia Nervosa, perhaps because of fears that it might compromise weight gain. Interestingly, in ballet dancers with reduced menstrual cycles (Young *et al.*, 1994) bone density in the hip (weight bearing) was preserved, while that in the spine (less weight bearing) was reduced, suggesting that weight bearing exercise might well be protective of bone in Anorexia Nervosa. Aside from encouraging weight gain, calcium and vitamin D intake and perhaps the use of drugs, the question of lifestyle change needs to be considered in a patient with severe osteoporosis (T-score $< -3$) which is staying the same or getting worse. The risk of fracture is elevated after minor trauma, and extra care on stairs, slippery paths and during activities such as bathing is advisable. Some intrepid patients ask if skiing, skateboarding and bungee jumping are advisable. My advice is that normal levels of BMI and bone mineral T-score are prerequisites for activities bearing a substantial risk of injury. Patients with vertebral collapse may suffer back pain which may require analgesics. Because patients inducing vomiting are at increased risk for gastro-oesophageal bleeding, aspirin-like drugs are best avoided. Equally, however, opioids such as codeine should be avoided because of lower GI effects and dependence so most analgesic drugs present problems.

*Gastrointestinal Problems    Dental attrition.* Teeth often suffer damage in eating disorders. (Milosevic, 1999). Vomiting exposes the enamel to gastric acid leading to erosion, and patients also consume acid drinks and fruits which contribute to the damage. In extreme cases, a few protruding fillings are all that remain of the original dentition. While acid digestion is probably the most important aetiological factor, others are at least theoretically of influence. Bingeing, when present, may expose teeth to high sugar foods which promote caries. Poor oral hygiene may be associated with changes in oral bacterial flora which may contribute, and vitamin deficiency disorders including scurvy can cause problems with teeth and gums. Receding gums occur in association with weight loss and vomiting while chewing food and spitting it out, which affects a proportion of patients with Anorexia Nervosa can damage tooth surfaces and lead to the temporomandibular joint (TMJ) syndrome.

### Patient Q

*A 26-year-old woman with a 12-year history of Anorexia Nervosa complained of pain in her right upper jaw. She was found by her dentist to have the TMJ syndrome. Her BMI was 15.5, and for the previous 4 years she had been spending several hours each day chewing food and spitting it out. The cost of this practice amounted to £300–400 (€ 500–700) each month. Her TMJ symptoms made the chewing painful but did not reduce it.*

Parotid enlargement also occurs in combination with both bingeing and vomiting, and may be a hypertrophic response to acid in the mouth or repetitive intense taste stimulation after prolonged restriction. Early on, it recedes when symptoms abate, but after years it may not go away quickly when bingeing and vomiting are controlled. Whether it becomes permanent is not known. The patient's appearance has been compared to that of a hamster with full cheek pouches, and the symptom has been confused with mumps. Patients checking their appearance may feel they have grown fatter and the result can be a redoubling of efforts to lose weight including vomiting which can, of course, make the parotid enlargement worse. Unfortunately, the appearance of parotid swelling in a patient with a long-standing eating disorder can add to stigma and alienation as well as dissatisfaction with her own appearance.

*Gastro-oesophageal reflux.* This is also an effect of prolonged self-induced vomiting. It appears that the lower oesophageal sphincter loses its competency allowing gastric contents to rise into the oesophagus, sometimes arriving in the throat. This has a number of effects. It makes self-induced vomiting much easier so that a patient who begins vomiting by putting her fingers down her throat, is able to vomit merely by leaning forward and increasing her intra-abdominal pressure. It this way, self-induced vomiting becomes much more of a natural activity, like eating, defecation or micturition, and hence more ego-syntonic. Arrival of gastric acid in the oesophagus causes irritation of the delicate mucosa with 'heartburn' and reflux oesophagitis. This can progress to more severe indigestion and pain in the chest or back. Bleeding also occurs, usually due to the same process, and this can be minor, leading in time to iron deficiency anaemia, or major, with vomiting of a large amount of blood (haematemesis) and collapse. Any bleeding should be taken seriously, and referral for endoscopy considered. If major referral to Accident and Emergency should be a matter of course both to diagnose other causes of bleeding such as gastro-duodenal ulceration and Mallory-Weiss syndrome (lower oesophageal tear due to vomiting) and to resuscitate the patient.

Lesser degrees of reflux oesophagitis in patients with bulimia nervosa can sometimes respond dramatically to high-dose proton pump inhibitor treatment (e.g. Zoton Fastab 30 mg bd). Sometimes, the regurgitation which accompanies reflux can also improve with this treatment. It should be added that refraining from vomiting for several weeks also improves reflux symptoms including pain and regurgitation.

*Colonic Problems    Laxative abuse: does it work to reduce nutrient absorption?*
Patients with eating disorders who abuse laxatives risk major short- and long-term problems. The first is that, in spite of their use by many people aiming to restrict the absorption of calories by their intestines, there is no good evidence that laxatives achieve this aim. There is very little research in this area and the only experimental studies of the effect of laxatives on absorption of nutrients in solution (Bo-Linn *et al.*, 1983) demonstrated only a modest reduction in absorption. However, many patients aver that the drugs cause recognizable chunks of food to appear in their stools. Moreover, protein-losing enteropathy has been described in patients with laxative abuse (Heizer *et al.*, 1968) and the question remains unresolved. Severe laxative abuse undoubtedly leads to dehydration, and that is accompanied by a satisfying, although illusory reduction in body weight. It also clears out

the colon, and can flatten the abdomen, another sought after but temporary effect, probably shared by colonic irrigation which has become a fashionable procedure.

*Other intestinal problems*    Many other chronic intestinal difficulties arise during the course of SEED. Colonic atony induced by long-term abuse of laxatives is associated with a 'floppy colon' which occurs because laxatives progressively damage the small nerves in the colonic wall, eventually impairing its contractility. In the early stages, reduction and cessation of laxatives leads to restoration of colonic function. However, after years of abuse, reduction of the dose results in severe constipation suggesting that the colon has become dependent on laxatives to function at all. Moreover, the 'floppy' colon may prolapse through the anus (rectal prolapse). The latter occurs as a result of colonic atony, together with wasting of the muscles of the pelvic floor and the effects of chronic constipation and prolonged 'pushing'. It may be associated with faecal and urinary incontinence.

The distended 'floppy' bowel can twist on itself (volvulus) leading to intestinal obstruction (abdominal pain and vomiting). However, the most unpleasant problem is chronic constipation. The nerves within the bowel wall are severely damaged, and eventually the bowel does not even respond to laxatives. It is useful to recruit the help of a gastroenterologist or surgeon to moderate the implementation of different approaches to the problems. These can include dietary changes (increasing fibre), the use of bulk and osmotic laxatives which do not damage the bowel as much as the irritant types, enemas, manual evacuation of faeces and, in extreme cases, surgical removal of non-functioning bowel sometimes with the provision of a colostomy.

*Endocrine Dysfunction    Infertility and amenorrhoea.* Amenorrhoea is usually associated with failure of ovulation and infertility. However, some women do menstruate, ovulate and become pregnant at low BMI, and the reasons are ill understood. Some women have normal ovarian function at low BMI. They may not have eating disorders and the phenomenon may be constitutional, for example in some ethnic groups such as South Asians, average weight may be lower and hence the low end of the Gaussian curve is shifted towards lower weights. It is of interest that, in India, 48% of the population are 'underweight' (BMI < 18.5) (Shetty and James, 1994) yet the total fertility rate (TFR) is 2.8 births per woman, compared to an underweight percentage of 4.9% in France and a European TFR of 1.5. Secondly, some women come from families in which low weight is common as a familial trait, with no other markers of eating disorders. These two examples of constitutional thinness, one ethnically determined, the other familial, do not require intervention, although they are sometimes referred to eating disorder clinics as 'possible eating disorders'. Once mother to daughter transmission of Anorexia Nervosa, either by genetic influences or underfeeding in childhood, has been eliminated there appears to be no further role for a psychiatrist.

A patient with Anorexia Nervosa may have menstruated at a low weight prior to onset of the illness, which may have indicated constitutional thinness or the gradual onset of the eating disorder. Moreover, some women with longstanding Anorexia Nervosa begin to menstruate and ovulate at a low BMI which can be under 16, much lower than their premorbid BMI. There may be a change in the hypothalamic setting for fertile cycles when weight is low for a long time, so that the patient begins menstruating at low weight. It is not known whether such low BMI cycling protects against osteoporosis and until this is settled, my practice is to ask patients to try and get their BMI above 18.5 if possible.

It will be clear that maintaining a low weight is not a reliable method of contraception, and if pregnancy is to be avoided precautions need to be taken in sexually active women. Some women with long-term Anorexia Nervosa and their partners are keen to have a baby and counselling about the possible risks and difficulties should be available through primary care, eating disorder and fertility services, preferably in communication with each other.

### Patient R

*A 34-year-old married woman with long-term Anorexia Nervosa discussed her wish to have a baby. She was advised in the eating disorders service that, at a BMI of 17 there were risks to the foetus and that she might find difficulties feeding the infant which could be addressed in psychological treatment. She consulted a privately practising fertility expert who gave her fertility enhancing medication. She became pregnant with twins who were born prematurely and were small for dates. Both babies died within a few days of birth.*

This case is related not to suggest that no woman with Anorexia Nervosa should ever be helped to conceive, but to indicate that the area is a risky one. This patient dropped out of eating disorder services follow-up which may have helped her gain some weight. Moreover, after the birth of a healthy baby, mothers with eating disorders may need substantial help around the time of weaning (Stein *et al.*, 2001).

*Oedema*   Swelling of lower limbs and, sometimes, of abdomen, can be a very challenging problem to a patient with a long-term eating disorder. As with many physical changes in the field the problem is poorly understood. It occurs most commonly in patients who have been underweight for a long time and are trying to gain weight and in those who habitually vomit or take laxatives or diuretics. It is thought that the body adjusts to the low blood pressure and total body sodium (reduced by poor intake and/or increased losses) by secreting a range of hormones which maintain blood pressure and conserve sodium. These include cortisol and aldosterone from the adrenal gland, angiotensin and renin from the kidney and antidiuretic hormone from the brain. The theory goes that high levels of some or all of these hormones (and others) are necessary to keep the patient from fainting and perhaps dying, and when she attempts to correct the abuses to her body by eating more (sometimes in the form of binges) or cutting down vomiting, laxatives or diuretics which mean more sodium stays in the body, the mechanisms described continue working for a while leading to an excess of sodium in the body. This could lead to oedema in two ways: by triggering heart failure in an underweight individual with compromised cardiac function (due to starvation) or by water, sodium and protein leaking out of the blood vessels which would occur if the latter had become more permeable or porous. The other likely outcome of sodium retention, namely raised blood pressure (arterial hypertension) does not seem to occur. This area is one that requires a substantial amount of research. Managing the problem is relatively straightforward, although not satisfactory. Increases in diet and withdrawal of laxatives and diuretics can be done gradually in a patient in whom oedema has been a problem. If it occurs again during treatment the changes in diet can be slowed and laxatives or diuretics introduced and reduced more slowly. If the oedema is intractable the possibility remains of using a diuretic that antagonizes aldosterone, such as spironolactone, following the theory that aldosterone levels may be raised in this situation. Using diuretics in a condition in which diuretic abuse is common raises concerns but the clinician may have little choice. Certainly, it would be appropriate to limit dosage and duration of therapy so that the patient does not become a long-term diuretic user.

# 4

# Social and Occupational Aspects
# of SEED

In this chapter, the difficulties encountered by people with eating disorders in social life, education, employment and other types of occupation will be considered. It may be thought that an eating disorder would have little impact and, in truth, many people suffering from long-term eating disorders have successful occupations, although their social lives, especially in relation to eating, are usually affected. However, when the effect of the eating disorder on mental life is pervasive, and when physical symptoms are severe, the disorders can have a profound impact and lead to substantial disability.

To start, two case histories will be related:

## Patient S

*This 37-year-old male patient was referred to an NHS day programme after spending over 2 years in a private inpatient and day care service funded by his local health purchaser, in an area where there was no specialist eating disorders service. Before discharge, he moved house to be in an area where there was such a unit. He developed Anorexia Nervosa after leaving school at the age of 18 when he went to university far from his home, to study engineering. He returned home and was admitted several times to local psychiatric units, where he gained some weight but did not receive psychotherapy. Several years after the onset, he was referred to a national centre for eating disorders where he received individual and family therapy and made some improvements, but relapsed rapidly after that treatment ended and he was referred back to local services. He moved away from home to live in a flat and was again treated by local services, and then referred to a private eating disorders centre in London where he spent a year as an inpatient and a further year as a day patient in a*

*Severe and Enduring Eating Disorder*   Paul Robinson
© 2009 John Wiley & Sons, Ltd

*hospital hostel before being referred on to the local NHS specialist service after he moved home to a hostel in London.*

### Patient Q

*This 43-year-old Afro-Caribbean woman was living with her mother and sisters. She had suffered from atypical Anorexia Nervosa, restricting type, since the age of 18 but had only been assessed as having an eating disorder at age 38. She had been working as an administrative assistant until 37 when she became depressed and suicidal following a minor injury (someone pulled her arm at an office party), and was hospitalized following major weight loss. She spent almost all her time at home, going out only for medical consultations. She would rise early in the morning and spend around 2 hours vacillating over what to wear. She would then begin thinking about what to eat and obsessive thoughts around food, calories and weight would last till the middle of the day into the afternoon. She would then tell herself 'if you've had to spend so long thinking about eating you can't really want to', and she would not eat or drink. She would sometimes sit and think nothing at all for several hours.*

*She has one friend she knows from primary school days. The friend phoned Patient Q every day and very occasionally, perhaps every 3 months, they meet for a coffee, although Patient Q will not have anything at those meetings. Patient Q's Anorexia Nervosa has been more severe over the last 7 years since her accident. Before that time, she was working and in a relationship which ended around the time of the accident. She has never been able to discuss her feelings about her difficulties and has shown no improvement with antidepressant medication.*

These two patients manifest many symptoms of SEED. They have a number of medical and psychiatric problems, Anorexia Nervosa, depression and obsessive compulsive symptoms for example, but also a number of difficulties in the social sphere, which will be the focus of this chapter and which are listed in Table 4.1.

## Accommodation

Both patients have a roof over their heads. However, for Patient S, accommodation is a problem, because as someone who is fastidiously clean and tidy, he finds it very difficult to share bathroom, toilet and kitchen with

Table 4.1  Some areas of social and occupational life affected in SEED

| Area | Difficulty | Possible response |
| --- | --- | --- |
| Accommodation | Fear of and wish for independence | Consider range of options with different levels of independence |
| Eating | Prolongation of meals, Eking behaviours, bingeing, eating out | Improve nutrition, practical help to minimize problem behaviours |
| Shopping | Food, clothes, shoplifting | Information, practice |
| Finances | State benefits, clinical frugality | Advice |
| Occupation | Training, interviews, high risk occupations, perfectionism | Advice, practice |
| Social network | Friendships, relationships | Activities, groups |
| Transport | Exercise, travel pass | Advice, monitoring |
| Orthocompulsions | Diet, exercise | Advice, monitoring |

others in a psychiatric hostel. He eats very little, and that little is further diminished when he finds evidence of heroin being prepared in the kitchen. He has attempted to obtain independent accommodation, but finds that he is low on the list for a transfer. Moreover, his low weight and continued anorexic and bulimic symptoms make him vulnerable living alone, and he has been considering supported accommodation which is even harder to obtain in his borough. Patient Q has accommodation with her family, which provides a certain amount of stability. However at 43 she had hoped to be more independent, and problems at home, including legal cases for violence against members of her close family, make living there stressful. She is also fearful of being alone and is not looking to move in the near future.

People with long-term eating disorders often have an ambivalent approach to independence, wanting to be separate from family and various support services yet subject to loneliness and feelings of abandonment, which seem to lead to recurrence of eating disorder symptoms and readmission to intensive treatment. Many patients say, 'If I get better no one will be interested.' So the search for the ideal level of supported accommodation can be a frustrating one. People with severe eating disorders sometimes behave as though the only time people really bother to think about them is when they are very seriously at risk. This makes planning support services very difficult. The patient may swing between 'I am an adult, and I need my own space and freedom like other people my age' and 'I am in extreme need but no one notices because my weight isn't too bad'. These psychological processes reflect difficulties in separation which may well in some patients extend back to problems in developing adequate attachments in childhood, although this statement is based on clinical impression rather than proper research.

These difficulties do not, however, apply to all patients and some can clearly cope with fully or semi-independent living with symptoms that are present but stable. The living arrangements that can be considered follow although some services are only currently available in some parts of the United Kingdom.

## Home with family

This is likely to be an option for younger patients as well as those with very longstanding SEED whose parents have become elderly and frail, in which case the patient may become a carer. The family will require support perhaps to change expectations if the eating disorder is unlikely to change substantially. Attendance at a family support group can help a family adjust to the difficult transition from an early eating disorder in which the hope and expectation is of change and perhaps recovery, to a later stage in which remaining the same is a major achievement.

## In independent accommodation with access to psychiatric and social services

This option provides varied outcomes, largely depending on the degree of community support available. The patient will have a care coordinator from the community mental health team (CMHT) and may also have a housing support worker. Her GP provides medication and medical monitoring while the consultant in the CMHT may provide support to other members of the professional network regarding assessment of eating disorder symptoms, depression, self-harm and other symptoms, and will call in specialists in these other fields as necessary. The patient may be deemed to be able to benefit from psychotherapy and, if so, a therapist may form part of the network. Because the group is diverse and complex, communication is essential as are regular meetings that may be 6 monthly. It is important to determine what changes in mental or physical state would occasion hospital admission, so that front-line workers know when to call in more senior members of the network to give an opinion on risk management.

### In a generic mental health hostel

This option may be considered because the patient is too frail or unstable to live on her own. Conditions in such hostels are often not conducive to maintenance of health for a number of reasons. The clientele is usually dominated by patients with chronic psychosis and a withdrawn, physically small, depressed patient can find the environment frightening and unsafe. Nevertheless some facilities, especially single sex female hostels, can be acceptable.

### Patient R

*A 26-year-old with a 12-year history of Anorexia Nervosa was unable to increase her BMI beyond 14 in hospital. She came from a part of the country with no local specialist eating disorder services, and a comprehensive support was arranged with the local psychiatric services along the lines suggested in the previous section. She was referred to a hostel with one sleep-in member of staff, a key worker with whom she met weekly and hostel groups 3 times weekly. Within the hostel, she had her own flat with food preparation and dining areas. The patient, who had not lived outside hospital for 7 years, successfully transferred to the hostel and did well for about 6 months. However, she then began to lose weight gradually and by 9 months she was back in hospital due to very low weight.*

This shows that a patient with SEED can be managed long-term as an outpatient as long as her eating and weight are stable, but if not, then admissions or at least intensive day care will be required from time to time.

### In a hostel exclusively for people with eating disorders

There are a few hostels catering exclusively for people with eating disorders, offering residential support and rehabilitation. As in the case of outpatients in hostels or independent accommodation, weight and physical risk factors should be stable. The placement in the hostel will generally be time limited, although the time may be substantial and patients should not pose a threat to their health from weight loss or risky behaviours. As in the generic mental health hostel, there will be key worker liaison with community psychiatric and eating disorder services. The major advantage of such a hostel is the understanding of the specific problems of eating disorders shared by staff and residents. SEED brings with it many problems such as difficulty buying clothes and food, and obsessive strictness over mealtimes. These and other specific difficulties, about which people with SEED often feel embarrassed, preferring to miss a meal which might be delayed rather than explain to staff, can be addressed and progress made in addressing them.

Because the referral rate for such services is likely to be low, partly because of difficulty in obtaining funding, hostels taking only people with eating disorders need to cover a large population, of the order of 5 to 10 million, and ideally they should have specific contracts for rehabilitation. They should also be evaluated in a controlled study against rehabilitation by local provision, including local eating disorder, general psychiatric and rehabilitation services.

## Eating

It is self-evident that people with SEED will have problems with eating. The areas of life affected are, however, surprisingly diverse. Buying food can be a nightmare for someone with an eating disorder. The modern practice of placing nutritional information on packets provides major grist to the obsessional mill. Obtaining the lowest calorie version of a particular yoghurt can take a substantial amount of searching. A discrepancy of, say, 2 cal between information given on one day rather than another, or in different parts of the packaging has, in at least one assertive patient, led to complaints to the manager and to the food production company. If there is doubt about which item is preferable, the person can become paralyzed by indecision and hours can pass with very little shopping being done. This behaviour, like many in Anorexia Nervosa, reflects real anxieties while at the same time, results in a reduction of food available for consumption and passes time in a calorie-free fashion.

Let us say that food is successfully purchased. Time can also drain away during preparation. Again there may be an underlying perhaps barely conscious directive to keep intake down. Food preparation, laying the table, getting the timing absolutely right, can all prolong the run up to a meal, restricting the time for actual eating.

**Patient Q**

*A 25-year-old with a long history of anorexia and bulimia nervosa was living with her family. She delayed her supper until 11 p.m., at which time she began preparations. She spent the next 2 hours cleaning, cutting and cooking the small quantity of vegetables destined for her supper. She then began preparing the table, cutlery and crockery. Her mother had been asked by her therapist to support her daughter's eating, so she dutifully remained on the scene while the patient engaged in her lengthy preprandial behaviours. By 2 a.m., when she at last sat down to eat, her mother could hardly stay awake for the actual meal which took a further 2 hours.*

This case history is extreme. However, it illustrates some of the problems in respect of eating faced by people with severe Anorexia Nervosa (and their exhausted carers). Extending the time taken to obtain, prepare and eat food can be part of a process which includes eating very slowly and cutting up food very small, which may be termed *eking behaviours* which may have the aim of restricting food intake, but also may be one of the behaviours accompanying starvation, making the food available last as long as possible. For bulimia nervosa (including those people with Anorexia Nervosa combined with bulimia), the problems are somewhat different. Like the patient with restrictive Anorexia Nervosa, she is constantly attempting to restrict her diet in order to achieve as low a weight as possible, or at least, keep weight gain under as much control as possible. At a certain point, often towards the evening, a different approach appears. Because of the enormous pressure to eat, as a result of undereating and underweight if it is present, the person is compelled to binge. This has the advantages of, at least temporarily satisfying food craving and, as the decision to binge has been made, the eating will be followed by vomiting, which will get rid of all or most of the food that has been ingested. Bingeing and vomiting can be rapid, but can also become a ritualistic series of behaviours that takes all day, and occupies the patient's time as effectively as restriction and the obsessional behaviour which can accompany it and which has been described above.

Eating disorder behaviours can, therefore, occupy much of the patient's time and leave little time for socializing. Indeed, patients often prioritize these behaviours over social activities, especially if the outing might involve food, as socializing so often does. Going out for a meal can be a major headache for a patient with restrictive Anorexia Nervosa, perhaps more than those with bulimic symptoms, as the latter group can eat and then compensate for what they have eaten by vomiting. Restaurants are very anxiety provoking, especially because the reassuring figures on the packet denoting calories and grams are absent and what is on the plate can only be judged by its approximate size and nutritional content. This means that any restaurant meal has to be strictly limited to foods such as salads, which can usually be relied upon to have low calorie content. Any sauce or gravy is out as are most desserts and, usually, alcoholic drinks. This makes life very restricted and, from a gastronomic point of view, boring. It is not surprising that people with eating disorders, especially restrictive Anorexia Nervosa, tend to refuse invitations for such outings and hence avoid the embarrassment of studying the menu and failing to find anything acceptable.

## Shopping

Buying clothing can also be a problem for a number of reasons. I have described above the supermarket paralysis that can occur when the person with an eating disorder is attempting to buy food and finds herself unable to choose between different varieties of similar foods. Clothes shopping is also very difficult. The patient perceives herself to be the wrong weight. She feels fat and may assume that others, including shop assistants, have the same view. If she is very underweight she may still feel fat but having been told *ad nauseam* that she is too thin, she may accept that to some degree. In this case, she now expects other people to regard her as abnormally thin and they may well express this view to her. This all makes clothes shopping something of a nightmare. Added to this are many patients' fear of seeing themselves in the mirror (although they may examine themselves frequently in the mirror in private to establish beyond doubt just how fat they are), and shopping becomes another activity to be avoided.

Some people with eating disorders have a tendency to shoplift. The origin of this and its frequency are not fully established, but it does appear to be more frequent than expected. Some patients steal food, and this could be understood as part of the psychological and behavioural response to starvation. An alternative explanation is simply that for a patient with bulimic symptoms, or someone who chews food and spits it out, food bills can be prohibitive and this could lead to a decision to steal food. Thirdly, some patients with Anorexia Nervosa hoard food. This is also thought to be related to starvation in a way similar to some animals' hoarding of food for the winter. Sometimes, a patient who hoards food will keep it unopened in her home. Depression and personality difficulties can also be behind stealing, in which case the stealing may be of non-food items, will often be of low value, and the individual may make no attempt to avoid being caught. It is questionable whether stealing non-food items is attributable directly to an eating disorder, and experts asked to report on patients charged with such offences will need to examine very carefully the link between the eating disorder and the stealing behaviour.

A further problem that besets patients with eating disorders, especially restrictive Anorexia Nervosa, is difficulty spending money, and this will be considered in the next section.

## Finances

Money can be a problem in a number of ways for a patient with a long-term eating disorder. While some patients are young women or men from families able to support them, this is not the case in the majority. Many patients are unemployed because of long-term disability, and may receive a not very generous government allowance called Disability Living Allowance as well as help with rent and other benefits. Occasionally patients will be allowed free travel, but this seems to depend on who is assessing the case.[1] Overall, patients can often just about cope financially. However, their disability may well be an expensive one, as indicated above, with a large regular expenditure on food for bingeing or, sometimes, for chewing food and spitting it out, which can run up very high food bills. At the other end of the scale is a feature, usually of the restricting form of Anorexia Nervosa, *clinical frugality*. In this, the patient is extremely reluctant to spend any money, and sometimes accumulates a fair sum in the bank by regularly saving income such as state benefits. The origin of this tendency is not clear. Some patients indicate that the wish to consume as little as possible, and that spending money on expensive clothes or gadgets cannot be justified as essential. It is as if the patient is trying to live on as little as possible, both in terms of food and other forms of consumption. Sometimes, electricity will

---

[1] Providers of reports should be aware that a free travel pass is more likely to be provided, if the patient has been declared unfit to drive. The latter can often be justified on the basis of hypoglycaemia, low blood pressure and cardiac effects of hypokalaemia.

be saved by turning the heating off and the resulting shivering may have the effect of burning off calories, and so satisfying the anorexic imperative. This attitude to consumption is, of course, in line with modern approaches to reduce global warming, and patients can have the additional satisfaction of knowing that their savings attract social approval. 'Hoarding' of money may be related to food hoarding, which is probably linked to undernutrition. Some patients comment that as they have a chronic illness, may not be able to work and have no supportive relatives they should save up as far as they can. Yet another motivation for avoiding spending is that of unworthiness. People with eating disorders often refuse food not only because they prefer to be thin, but because they feel unworthy of food, goodness, enjoyment, in fact anything positive. This is, of course, consistent with the patient's low self-esteem which may come from a number of sources: childhood abuse, failure to establish positive relationships or perhaps a problem which has its source in the patient's innate characteristics which would be manifest whatever the person's life experience. Reluctance to receive anything good predicts that spending money would be a problem, and patient's comments about their frugality supports this notion. The result of frugality is that the patient may live a life devoid of pleasurable activities or acquisitions, something like a Trappist Monk who embraces austerity and so avoids materialistic diversions. The patient with SEED may reach the point of independence of many aspects of the material world. She may, however, experience unpleasant problems with her skin, because of reluctance to use any form of moisturizer or other creams, and introduction to these aspects of self-nurturing (e.g. in the course of massage therapy) can significantly improve quality of life.

## Occupation

As has been seen, an eating disorder can be a major impediment to social interaction, and itself become a full-time occupation. When faced with the question 'How would you anticipate spending your day time?' some patients become anxious and conclude that their eating disorder is so absorbing that they could not imagine having an occupation as well! Parkinson's law[2] applies to both the symptoms and the occupation. If left with no occupation, there will be little impediment to the symptoms expanding to fill the entire

---

[2]'Work expands to fill the time available for its completion'.

day, while if an occupation is taken up, it may reduce the space available for the symptoms. Many patients are, however, able to bring their symptoms under enough control to contemplate work and in some professions the energy, enthusiasm and lack of alternative activities (outside the eating disorder) can be advantages. If a patient with SEED has a stable physical state, work may continue as usual.

### Patient S

*A patient of 44 with longstanding Anorexia Nervosa since the age of 18 worked as a coordinator in a prestigious academic journal. She had marked obsessional and perfectionistic traits, which were reflected in her work which was of a very high standard. She maintained a BMI of around 12.9 and required occasional admissions to correct reductions in her weight. When her mother became ill she helped her father nurse her at home, and she subsequently nursed and supported her father when he developed cancer. She was highly respected and valued at work, although she required hospital care every year or two when her physical state demanded. Her clinical care included weekly monitoring in the eating disorders service and in primary care, alternately, and consisted of BMI, SUSS test, bloods for urea and electrolytes and liver function tests and an ECG. When her weight fell, as it did over the time of her mother's illness and death, the question of admission was raised, but she was able to pull her weight up so that she avoided the dreaded hospital bed.*

This history shows that severe SEED can be compatible with a successful work life. It is uncertain what factors in the patient, the family and the illness make this possible. This particular patient indicated that she had a warm, loving relationship with her parents, and that the origins of the eating disorder might have been related to an episode of abuse that she had alluded to but had never been able to discuss. Her treatment required close monitoring and medical intervention as necessary, much as one might manage the health of someone with diabetes mellitus or systemic lupus. Some occupations, such as ballet or modelling, place very substantial pressure on the individual to remain underweight, and if she cannot be persuaded to accept a different area of work, the outcome may be a longstanding eating disorder. Sometimes, it is possible to liaise with medical services attached to a ballet school or even a modelling agency, and request that less pressure be applied, and some organizations have been subject to intense adverse publicity (Hall, 2000). Probably, the most powerful medium of change lies within the organization itself. For example, the Italian government was able to ban underweight models (BMI <18.5) from the catwalks in 2006 (McMahon, 2006).

For the patient with no occupation, a danger is often that she will see herself not as ill but as inadequate, and that she should be doing the same training or employment as others her age. As a result, she may refuse any occupation that she sees as 'lesser' such as a work environment for people who have suffered psychiatric illness. She may end up not doing anything as a result, trapped by her perfectionist dichotomous reasoning, 'I can't do it perfectly so I won't do it at all.'

For someone who is able to transcend these dispiriting processes, perhaps aided by therapy, and feels able to begin the process of occupational rehabilitation the first step is to discuss in the light of her interests and experience what area might be suitable. A patient who has been a doctor, for example, might be able to go back to medicine, but may also benefit from the experience of working as a volunteer in order to reintroduce herself to the work environment and build up the necessary confidence to return to her previous role. Moreover, going back onto the career ladder may bring with it the worry that the return has to be successful, as difficulties may be observed by colleagues and supervisors and might even lead to training contracts being withdrawn.

Because eating disorders often strike during adolescence, those with the most severe and long-lasting disorders may find themselves lacking a specific training, and may well need to think about registering for courses in an area of interest. Someone who has developed Anorexia Nervosa at 13, struggled through examinations and then reached 25 with a lot of experience of life as a psychiatric patient, but little else, will find herself in the same position as someone of 18 who is very uncertain about what to do as a career. The knowledge that many people without eating disorders, having left university with an increased understanding of one or two subjects but little specific training suitable for a job, feel the same way may be some comfort. Some people with an eating disorder do have a skill at which they excelled, but might be reluctant to exploit it because of the negative associations they may have with overwork, perfectionism and excessive expectations in relation to the particular skill. In contrast to the area of excellence, however, other pursuits may seem drab and uninviting.

### Patient Q

*A woman of 25 had been an excellent artist at school, and had been predicted to make a career in fine art. She developed her eating disorder in early adolescence, and by the time she was able to maintain a low but stable weight which allowed her to avoid hospital admission, she was 24 and reluctant to engage in drawing because of the imperfections she was able to discern, having avoided art during her acute illness. She explained further that she loved drawing, and did not wish to make it something by which she was judged, and by which she judged herself.*

These are problems that cannot be resolved easily. The above attitudes may well be part of a general tendency to perfectionism and self-criticism that could be addressed directly using cognitive behavioural methods. The stages of change that are required are first, to make a realistic assessment of capabilities, secondly to help the patient overcome impediments to action, for example by using cognitive behavioural techniques to challenge unhelpful dichotomous reasoning and clinical perfectionism, as described above. The patient then has a view of what she can do, and needs to make a choice from what is available. Localities do vary, and the ideal service is one which welcomes people who have received treatment for psychiatric problems, which makes reasonable demands, for example on times of attendance, but has some flexibility bearing in mind fluctuations in motivation that can occur in people with psychological difficulties. The patient should have an identified key worker who is in contact with the psychiatric team, and the unit should offer a wide range of activities encompassing most levels of ability. In such a workshop, which functions as a commercial printer, activities include preparing orders for dispatch, printing and the use of both word processing and graphic design software in order to produce the required product. Most patients will find a niche within that range, although the highest fliers might find that there remains a substantial gap between the most complex tasks that the workshop can offer and their accustomed level of functioning.

For a patient who already has a job, the process of return to that employment can present challenges. Added to the problems of perfectionism and dichotomous reasoning, are the concern that colleagues and managers will have seen the patient before (perhaps at a different weight) and the patient will be acutely conscious (often but not always unrealistically) of their thinking about her, whether she is coping, having symptoms of illness, fat, failing and so on. Again, these concerns can be approached using cognitive behavioural techniques and the return to work managed by the team helping the patient design an appropriate plan. The return to work needs to be at a realistic rate, for example starting at 1 to 3 half days, and building up to the target over an agreed time, say, 1 to 3 months. Sessions with the mental health worker should continue at least weekly during this phase, and difficulties identified and addressed. Probably, the most important element of therapy is support and recognition of the difficulty of the process. Sometimes the nature of the work needs to be addressed, so that initially less demanding tasks are required, or the patient may shadow a person covering her role for a while. All this requires substantial cooperation from the employer, and a proportion are willing to make the required arrangements, as long as reports from the treating team provide detail on both the work that can be expected and, most importantly, a time frame for return. Sometimes, the patient will report that she is expected to be back at work full time within a week. Contact with the employer can sometimes mitigate this demand. Larger employers, including public bodies such as the National Health Service, are usually more able to be flexible than small private companies, indeed they are bound by their own policies to be so. Patients who lose their jobs because of illness may have a case under employment law, and can be directed to sources of legal advice.

Getting time off work for therapy sessions is usually possible, although patients who have just started a job, and those who wish to conceal their medical condition from their employer, may not wish to do so, in which case sessions may be offered outside office hours, although this is not universally available in NHS services. If a letter is required for employers, some patients request that it be made from a general hospital without mention of mental health or eating disorders, although with the rise of UK mental health trusts, often in separate buildings, this service is becoming increasingly difficult to provide.

Job interviews present another ordeal for the patient with a history. Her appearance may or may not give a clue to her illness. How does she explain the gaps in her CV? Does she tell all or does she obfuscate with a reference to 'lengthy treatment for a serious condition'? Some employers, and even organizations do exhibit stigma to psychiatric disorder, and we professionals cannot pretend otherwise. The NHS in the past, as a result of the conviction of a murderous nurse with major personality problems as well as bulimia, made it very difficult for people with a history of an eating disorder to be taken on as student nurses, leading a number to fail to mention this in their medical histories. Appearance is also an important factor to consider prior to interview. As we have seen, shopping, especially for clothes is very difficult, and patients, both male and female, may need specific help in choosing a good outfit for the interview.

# Social Network

*Coming for a bite? See you at the pub. We're going to Carlucci's to give Trish a real send off! Would you like to come up for a coffee? Come for brunch. We're having a Barbie. Do come for tea! The Lord Chamberlain is commanded by Her Majesty to invite . . . Tea for two. Breakfast at Tiffany's. The Dinner Party. Mars, for work rest and play. The lady loves . . . Milk Tray.*

Little that is social can happen without that four-letter word food. People with eating disorders might just about manage to organize their buying, preparing and consuming food on their own. As soon as a person without an eating disorder is involved, the whole project becomes very complicated. The priorities for the patient remain to control food intake, minimize calories and keep, or preferably push, weight down. In practice that means that social life is difficult. A meal at a restaurant means, firstly, a menu which is often unfamiliar, dishes whose contents are not absolutely known, weird sauces that have all sorts of cal-horrific things in them. In brief, loss of control, the patient's nightmare. She is hiding behind the giant menu attempting to choose something and getting into a major panic. She ends up choosing a mixed salad with no dressing with a glass of water, which is a signal for everyone else to look sympathetically and return to deciding between a Veneziana or a Quattro Stagione. The bulimic option is one way out of this public humiliation, but disappearing to the toilet is also a sign to those who know that what goes down must come up, and cover is almost equally blown. No surprise, therefore that the long list of social occasions in which food (and/or alcohol) consumption is required becomes a list of occasions to be avoided with the result that people with eating disorders, especially where the disorder is publicly apparent, become socially isolated. This is probably more of an issue for people with Anorexia Nervosa, whether restricting or bulimic. People with normal weight bulimia nervosa often manage to maintain a reasonably satisfactory social life unless their bulimia is so frequent and time consuming that it takes over time allotted to social encounters, so that invitations from friends are refused because the patient is due to binge then. This conveys the important message that bulimia is a more attractive companion than a human friend.

A set of barriers even greater in number and height stand in the way of sexual relationships. The restrictions on eating argue against any romantic activity in which food is an accompaniment or a prelude. Libido is often reduced in Anorexia Nervosa due to weight loss, while low self-esteem, appalling body image, reduced physical sexual responses and the effect of previous, sometimes unwanted and adverse sexual experiences, make a physical relationship quite a remote possibility. This is particularly poignant in someone who is desperate for a caring, intimate relationship such as can be provided in a loving sexual union.

Many people with long-term eating disorders have a small social circle, reduced to one or two very close, usually female friends who know and accept the problems, and not infrequently, have experienced eating difficulties themselves.

Social isolation in eating disorders, as well as in other long-term psychiatric disorders, is a significant problem which needs to be addressed, but in which answers are not simple. The therapeutic relationship with the key worker or therapist is one way in which a relationship can be trialled with someone who is reliable, accepting, supportive (yet willing to challenge appropriately) and non-threatening. The relationship is not and can never be sexual, and those therapists and other health care workers who exploit their power by engaging in sexual activity are rightly disbarred from practice when discovered. Within the therapeutic sessions, the patient can gain confidence in relating to another individual who knows about the eating problems, and yet is accepting. Apart from therapists, patients often feel least threatened by other people with eating disorders, although those that are 'thinner than me' (i.e. everyone) are often the subject of envy. Therapeutic groups, and perhaps more social groups can represent an important step in resocialization. A therapist can take a group of patients for a coffee, to practice choosing and ordering in a restaurant, and to engage socially. A possible next step might be for two or three patients to go out together. A group of patients living together is not uncommon and might be seen as a prelude to work and educational steps, voluntary work and activity and interest groups, more contact with the general population, and perhaps, the beginnings of social activities with people who are neither therapists nor people with eating disorders. Following a discussion along the lines given above, a patient may wish to take each scenario described, perhaps add some of her own, and place them in a list with the least threatening first, and the most threatening last, which gives a hierarchy of feared social situations and an order in which to address them.

# Transport

Getting about is a problem mainly in that it is a common way for people with eating disorders to expend energy in order to keep weight down. Those with Anorexia Nervosa may push themselves to the limit before acknowledging that their muscle power has declined due to weight loss.

### Patient T

*A woman of 29 with Anorexia Nervosa was living with her mother who would receive breakfast in bed each morning. As the patient's weight fell, her muscle power reduced, and she became unable to get up the stairs holding the tray. She would, therefore, place the tray on the next step and use all her effort to haul her body up the step, before grasping the tray and placing it on the next higher step. In this way, she gradually made her way up the stairs and continued to give her mother breakfast in bed.*

The individual who has a chronically low body weight may only need to lose a small amount, say, 2–3 kg, to experience very serious consequences with muscle weakness, liver problems and the other potentially fatal changes documented in Chapter 3. The balance between nutrition, body weight and exercise may be a fine one. The low weight individual needs to eat less to maintain a particular body weight, but that figure will be compromised by any substantial amount of exercise of moderate or low intensity (such as walking). To provide some figures.

A woman of 30 has chronic Anorexia Nervosa, with a weight of 40 kg and a BMI of 14.8. She decides to save money by walking to work for 40 minutes twice daily. What is the implication for her nutritional state?

### Calorie requirements

The Harris–Benedict equation gives us a rough idea of her basal requirements (without any activity at all) (see Figure 4.1 ). This gives a calorie requirement for the patient of 1203 kcal per day. Multiply by 1.2, for minimal exercise gives 1443 kcal per day.

Men: BMR $= 66 + (13.7 \times W) + (5 \times H) - (6.8 \times \text{Age}) = $ Daily calories required

Women: BMR $= 665 + (9.6 \times W) + (18 \times H) - (4.7 \times \text{Age}) = $ Daily calorie needs

Multiply BMR by an exercise factor for different activity levels:

Sedentary – no or very little exercise: $1.2\times$

Light activity for average of 2 days/week: $1.375\times$

Moderate activity level exercising 4 days/week: $1.5\times$

High activity levels exercise and sports 7 days/week: $1.7\times$

Higher activity levels: up to $2\times$

Woman of 40 kg, 1.64 m, 30 yr needs 1203 kcal/d BMI 14.8

Woman of 55 kg, 1.64 m, 30 yr needs 1347 kcal/d BMI 20.4

Where:

$W = $ weight (kg)

Height (cm)

Age $= $ Years (yr)

**Figure 4.1** The Harris–Benedict equation.

## Excess calories expended through walking

Walking is thought to expend about 80 cal per 20 minutes, which amounts to 320 cal extra per day.

## Extra food required to avoid weight loss

Taking the standard slice of white bread as our currency (it is not too hard to convert it mentally to rice or pasta), each slice gives about 80 cal, so our patient will need to eat extra 4 slices of bread per day.

This graphically illustrates the knife edge that the patient is on. If she does not make the necessary changes in diet (not unlikely), then within 3 months she will have lost 3.84 kg (a reduction of 1000 kcal per day leads on average to weight loss of roughly 1 kg per week, so a deficit of 320 kcal per day leads to an estimated loss of 0.32 kg per week), her BMI will be 13.4 and she may well be heading for a hospital admission.

How can we help someone who has an anorexic gremlin following her or him around saying 'Do more, eat less, be thinner' repeatedly and incessantly? Just as the drug addict is pursuing chemical *Nirvana*, no matter what the cost, so is the Anorexia Nervosa sufferer pursuing thinness whatever the cost. As professionals, our hope is that, by making the patient fully aware of the cost, in terms of physical and mental symptoms, need for hospital care, loss of freedom and access to usual activities, she will make the difficult decision to defy the gremlin and ignore its exhortations. Accordingly, exercise can be seen as another way to restrict weight that must be balanced by increasing dietary intake. The additional diet must be adequate, and the calculations above can help introduce some realistic quantities to what is being proposed, for example in a meal plan discussion.

In contrast to the public image of people with eating disorders as well-to-do, many with long-term conditions are, as indicated in this chapter, short of money. That can be because they are unable to work due to the effects of the eating disorder on their careers. In addition, however, people with bulimic binges may spend a large amount of money on food, and have few financial reserves on which to call. It is sometimes possible, in areas with understanding assessors, to obtain free travel passes for people with eating disorders who are addicted to exercise, and this can be a helpful provision for someone who is ambivalent about restricting exercise. Spending on transport may be seen by the patient as bad for a number of reasons: it misses an opportunity for weight control, it costs money, which offends the patient's 'hoarding instinct' mentioned above, and exercise (like weight loss) is continually and increasingly advised and advertised by health experts so it must be good for you!

## Orthocompulsive Disorder: Obsessed with Doing the Right Thing!

Social norms may have a major impact on people with SEED. Their symptoms, to a health care professional, may appear profoundly unhealthy. However, when seen in the context of well-publicized campaigns to improve the nation's health through increasing exercise, decreasing calorie intake, weight reduction, reducing body fat and blood fat content, reducing sugar consumption and the rest, the patient with an eating disorder may well feel that she or he is following professional advice and adopting a healthy lifestyle. Hence, when a patient with a BMI of 14 claims to eat 'only healthy food', meaning fruit, vegetables, salad and spring water, she has the entire healthy eating industry behind her. The fact that she is patently unhealthy, because she is on a weight reducing diet, is seen as quibbling and anti-health. The presence of socially prescribed health preoccupations to an unhealthy degree is often seen in eating disorders, and can be termed *orthocompulsions* (*ortho* meaning correct). *Orthocompulsions* suggest an extreme urge to comply with recommended behaviour to a degree that damages health. Thus, eating 'healthily' to the point of death from malnutrition or exercising (including low impact, moderately intensive exercise such as walking) which results in physical damage would be included. The former might be applied to someone following a diet which led to vitamin deficiency, while the latter could cover compulsive exercise which leads to muscle development in women and fat reduction, so that osteoporosis is one outcome. Also included would be keeping weight down to a point at which binge eating occurred. Such a patient would fulfil criteria for bulimia nervosa. This term also raises the possibility that some people with *orthocompulsions* whose problems did not come under the eating disorder umbrella might be regarded as suffering from a mental disorder (*orthocompulsive disorder*) if there were serious consequences of their behaviour such as those suggested above. The concept overlaps with *orthorexia nervosa* (Bratman and Knight, 2001). The advantage of the *orthocompulsive* label is that it does not identify so closely with eating disorders.

# 5

# Family Life with SEED

**Lunch: A Short Play**

SHEILA:  Have you finished in the kitchen, darling, I just need to get in for a minute to get lunch for me and Daddy.

NATALIE: I won't be much longer.

SHEILA:  You have been there for a couple of hours and I really do need to . . . .

NATALIE: Well if you don't want me to eat at all, fine.

SHEILA:  Of course I do. Take as long as you need.

*The lunch table an hour later*

PETER:    How's the work going for the exams?

NATALIE: OK, Dad. I wish I'd dropped Chinese, though, it's so hard.

PETER:    I'm sure you'll be OK. (beat) That looks a bit meagre, if you're supposed to be putting on weight. Would you like some bread?

NATALIE: *Cries and runs out*

SHEILA:  Oh, Peter, how could you. You know how sensitive she is. Now she'll just go and walk for miles and miss out her snack.

PETER:    Did you see what she'd made? Lettuce and carrot covered in vinegar and pepper. Am I supposed to say nothing while she looks like death?

*Severe and Enduring Eating Disorder*   Paul Robinson
© 2009 John Wiley & Sons, Ltd

## Living with Family of Origin

Someone with a chronic eating disorder may well continue to live with her parents in the long term. She may be the only child left at home, siblings having established homes and partnerships away. As the family ages, parents may come to accept that for the time being their son or daughter is not likely to leave the illness behind. As long as this occurs, relationships can be more equitable than before. Parents also need to be reassured that monitoring is in place to detect any dangerous changes in physical state, for example in body weight or blood tests. In this setting, with perhaps reluctant acceptance by parents that SEED has made its appearance together with fair stability and adequate medical monitoring of the eating disorder, life can proceed reasonably satisfactorily. Under the surface, both family and sufferer may harbour grief for the lost person that might have been without the eating disorder, but that grief is rarely expressed. In this acceptance scenario, re-lationships in the family can become less distorted. In a family in which the wish for change is constantly expressed, especially at mealtimes, as in the short play at the head of the chapter, a number of tensions can arise. Years of eating disorder may have lead to an extremely close and concerned relationship between mother and daughter or son. Occasionally, it is the father who is recruited to be the close monitor of the sufferer's eating, ex-ercise, purging, weight and all the other indicators of health and illness. In a condition which can be fatal the parents' desire to monitor closely is not all that surprising. When the mother is the close monitor, the father will often monitor from a distance, commenting on weight and eating without the detailed knowledge that is the province of his wife. The close association between the mother and sufferer can lead to the father distancing himself from what he may perceive as the 'women's issues' around food, eating, body image and menstruation. This can manifest in his spending more and more time away, working late, travelling on business and sometimes having rela-tionships away from home, sexual or otherwise. Communication between the parents often deteriorates and the relationship can become increasingly distant.

Most families in which this occurs recognize that it is unhealthy. It may perpetuate dependence of daughter on mother and vice versa, so that trips away are very difficult for the couple. This is a situation in which fam-ily therapy to help the mother disengage from the offspring with long-term Anorexia Nervosa is very important, and this will be covered later in the chapter. Janet Treasure, Professor of Eating Disorders Psychiatry at the Maudsley Hospital, has very creatively produced animal metaphors (http://www.iop.kcl.ac.uk/sites/edu/downloads/flyer_family.pdf) to indicate the roles that carers find themselves adopting, while health care professionals are not immune from these roles, themselves! The Carer Metaphorical Menagerie includes the following beasts:

The kangaroo: the overprotecting carer.

The rhinoceros: storming in and making a terrific noise about the patient's behaviour (a role favoured by fathers, but not exclusively their preserve).

The ostrich: denying the problems.

The jellyfish: overwhelmed by their emotional response to the problem.

The dolphin (one of the more useful ways to cope, if you can do it): swims alongside and gives the occasional nudge with his/her nose to encourage the patient in the right direction.

The St Bernard (another good one): calm, always there, dedicated, bringing nurture and sustenance to those lost in the snow.

Carers will surely recognize themselves and their partners in this list, sometimes being one animal and sometimes another. The descriptions of family therapy for Anorexia Nervosa by Minuchin (1990) and Russell *et al.* (1987), however, suggests an approach which is reflected in none of these animals, a parent who insists on change in spite of protests, screams and the rest, and who does not stop until the changes are achieved. Two creatures that spring to mind are a British Bulldog and a Yorkshire Terrier.

If the person with the eating disorder remains until the parents are elderly, she may find herself in the role of the carer of a parent who may have become ill with a stroke or cancer. For the daughter whose life may have been one of disability requiring care herself, this can be a time which although distressing may bring rewards, and a closeness with parents can ensue based on gratitude that the daughter is actually around and not raising three children in another continent like her sister. The extra strain of caring for a relative must be borne in mind by medical services, because if deterioration or death of a parent occurs the accompanying grief may be expressed as weight loss and physical disability. Indeed, a person with an eating disorder, who has become very close to a parent, may harbour the intention of dying at the same time as or soon after the parent.

## Living Away from the Family

In Western Europe and similar societies the combined influences of prosperity and individualism, as well as young women benefiting from increasingly liberal attitudes to girls in some cultures, have led to an expectation that after leaving school a young person can expect to move away from home, whether with other young people in a shared home or a university campus or increasingly abroad. Difficulty funding affordable housing has to some extent reversed the trend, and has led to unplanned appearances of unemployed, homeless graduates on the parents' doorstep accompanied by a large rucksack.

For someone who has struggled to keep alive throughout adolescence in order to achieve the place at the top university, leaving home can be a major ordeal. For people who are the subject of this book, and have been seriously ill for 10 years or more and required major therapeutic intervention, it is even more onerous. Consider a young person who has developed Anorexia Nervosa at 13, been in and out of hospital for several years, and at 18 managed to maintain a low but survivable weight, and by 24 has obtained the necessary qualifications to go to university. She expresses determination to go or her life will be meaningless. However, her parents, used to a life of recurrent crises, are doubtful she will cope. How can they support her at a distance so that she will manage to survive away from home? The patient may assert that the only place offering a particular combination of philosophy and animal psychology is in a university with no specialist eating disorder services for 200 miles. That may be a survivable problem as the main intervention will be medical monitoring and general psychological support, although the services of a knowledgeable dietician may also be useful. The local primary care service needs to know when to call in the medical and psychiatric services. However, because of the frequency of eating disorders in students, many student health services are proficient at monitoring and appropriately referring.

Managing at home can be difficult when the offspring is away. Daily phone-calls are routine and parents feel even more powerless than usual. Someone with a very long-term eating disorder, who is stabilized at home and manages to maintain weight away from home, runs the risk of social isolation and excessive working with accompanying depression. As in the case of the person with an eating disorder living at home, the aim is for the young person to adapt by using services such as the student health service and local dietetic and therapy services, and depend less on home. Therapy for the family during this phase can address this often difficult transition. A model of the eating disorder which includes insecure attachment (see Table 5.1) can be very helpful in understanding these difficulties, although it may only apply to a proportion of patients (Ward *et al.*, 2001). The growing child has difficulties with primary attachments (mother, father) for some reason, which could be inside or outside the family, or even a developmental problem (e.g. autistic spectrum disorders). This leads to poor self-image, perfectionism and poor mentalizing capacity. As long as the child is in a structured environment in which expectations are very clear (examinations etc.) and support structures are close by (i.e. living at home), little problem is noticed. However, when the possibility of separation is apparent (approaching 'gap year', moving away, having a first relationship), the child retreats from adult development by self-starvation and weight loss, achieving another social approved goal. The child fails to separate because of the dangerous nature of the eating disorder, which elicits extreme examples of caring behaviour in parents. Fast forwarding several years, after attempts at treatment including long hospital admissions, the child, now chronologically an adult, has SEED, and is trying to separate. The original attachment issues remain unresolved, and the repeated episodes of illness with high parental anxiety and increased dependence of the child on parents and their proxies (e.g. eating disorder services) may have made separation even more difficult to achieve. The result is that attempts to move away to reconnect with a career path perhaps through education become extremely difficult, and can result in the return of dangerous deterioration in symptoms.

Living in the same town as parents, in a flat or house-share, brings a different set of difficulties. If, as is usually the case, the individual brings with her behaviours around food that others will find odd, if not annoying, the effects on her house-mates will need to be taken into account. Storage of particular types of food (e.g. vegan, low calorie) in larder and fridge does not usually cause problems as long as they are labelled properly. Eating a different diet in a house in which people generally eat at separate times is also not problematic. However, for someone with bulimic symptoms, taking food from house-mates' stores is rarely tolerated, even if coins to the value of the food taken are left by the container. Purging behaviour, such as vomiting, can cause problems if house-mates become aware of the behaviours through smell, but most sufferers, if careful, are able to conceal the evidence.

**Table 5.1**  A theoretical attachment model of eating disorder tracing attachment and symptoms through different stages of the condition and life cycle

|  | Secure | Insecure |
| --- | --- | --- |
| Initial attachment to caregivers | Secure | Insecure |
| School years | Child with parents. Does well at school. System holds together. | Child with parents. Does well at school. System holds together. |
| Late adolescence: Moving away (gap year, first relationship, higher education) | Adolescent moves away emotionally and/or geographically. Supported by parents. Establishes own life away. | Adolescent tries to move away but separation anxiety leads to continued extreme dependence on parents, perhaps an eating disorder. |
| Early adulthood | Young adult is living away with occasional visits, phone calls, crisis calls. | Young adult is away but always a cause for concern through frequent calls, visits, crises, health problems. |
| Mid adulthood | Adult established away with potential support. Parents use her old room as an office and then hitch hike to Mongolia. | Adult is away but health crises lead to hospital admissions and may occasion return home. |
| Later adulthood | Grandchild arrives. Renewed needs for support. Parents long back from Mongolia | Long-term eating disorder (SEED). Health monitoring in place. Reasonable calm. Close support by parents. Adult patient supports parents' crises. |

Someone who maintains a low weight can be a source of concern to friends and house-mates who may come to a clinic with their ill cohabitee. Their problem is more usually that they can only have a partial understanding of the problem, and therefore may worry unnecessarily. Moreover, some friends and house-mates may take on the care of someone looking frail and vulnerable in a way that can be unhealthy both for the sufferer, who is attempting to establish independence, and the supporter who may be acting out of his or her own need to be in charge of, and the saviour of, a dependent and ill person.

With these caveats in mind, it may be useful to offer sessions to a patient, together with a friend or house-mate, and help both establish appropriate boundaries for each other and between the patient and home. This accords with the advice often given in self-help texts to recruit a 'buddy' who knows about the eating disorder and can act as a support and confidante while the patient accesses treatment.

## Living in a Family of Creation

This is yet another scenario, and a common one for older patients, who are living with a boyfriend, a husband (or girlfriend/wife) and possibly children. In someone with a long-term eating disorder, it is likely that the relationship developed while the eating disorder was present. This is not necessarily the case and in some cases the eating disorder developed during the relationship. However, the eating disorder may have been concealed from the partner for years, the patient being frightened in case discovery of the truth will break up the relationship. This is particularly likely in eating disorders in which weight loss is not severe, and bulimic episodes and vomiting are the main symptoms. The patient who may have been heavier in the past becomes trapped by the belief that if she gives up her eating disorder, e.g. stopping vomiting after eating, she will regain weight to its previous level, and the relationship, reliant on her remaining very slim, will fail. She may come for therapy without her partner's knowledge, wanting to give up bingeing and vomiting, but not to gain any weight. This might be possible, but it is more likely to be difficult to achieve. The vomiting may be acting as an overflow valve in a tank which keeps water at a certain level. Disable the valve and the water level (i.e. body weight) rises.

Secondly, in a couple in which one has an eating disorder, the partner may well have similar issues about body weight and even an eating disorder, although this may not be known to the patient. Couples may be drawn to each other because of a common interest in health and fitness, and may have met in a health club.

*Patient U*

*A patient with bulimia nervosa attended a couples group. In the first session, her partner disclosed that he was very body conscious, constantly trying to reduce his weight and binged regularly. The revelation proved too much for the relationship which broke up shortly after.*

## Children of Women with Chronic Eating Disorders

There has been a fair amount written about the offspring of women with eating disorders, especially Anorexia Nervosa but also severe bulimia nervosa. There is an increased risk of malnutrition during pregnancy (Kouba *et al.*, 2005; Morgan, Lacey and Chung, 2006). There is an increase in controlling behaviours in the eating disordered mothers of 1-year-olds (Stein *et al.*, 2001), and children may be in danger of growth-retardation and possible eating disorders later on (Hodes, Timimi and Robinson, 1997; Whelan and Cooper, 2000). In view of all this, women with chronic eating disorders should, along with their partners, receive full information and counselling over these issues, and if the couple decide to go ahead, they should receive substantial support during and after the birth. It is arguable whether women with longstanding mild Anorexia Nervosa should be given assisted fertility treatment. They should at least have a trial of therapy for their eating disorder beforehand so as to provide the best possible opportunity for a healthy outcome over the pregnancy. Although there is an increased rate of foetal malnutrition and stillbirth in the pregnancies of women with Anorexia Nervosa, the rate has not very much increased and the majority of infants are born healthy. The mother's body appears to prioritize the nutrition of the baby over the mother, so that even if she undereats the baby may grow well and progress should be monitored with foetal ultrasound measurements. Nevertheless, dietetic advice is helpful and vitamin and mineral supplements, as well as the usual iron and folate are sensible.

There may be a slight increase in birth defects (cleft pallet) and multiple births in the offspring of women with normal weight bulimia, although this finding remains to be replicated (Lacey and Smith, 1987). In fact, most women with bulimia nervosa manage to reduce or eliminate their bulimic symptoms during the pregnancy, with a majority relapsing in the puerperium.

Feeding the baby initially may be unproblematic. Patients with eating disorders often value the natural purging of calories that occurs through breast feeding, and they may lose more weight during this time than a non-eating disordered woman might.

Weaning can, however, bring problems as Stein *et al.* (2001) have convincingly shown. While non-feeding activities appear unaffected, mealtimes are fraught. Eating disordered mothers may have difficulty judging their baby's size (feeling they are fatter than they are) and nutritional needs, sometimes overfeeding and sometimes underfeeding. Additionally, some mothers have quite phobic attitudes to food, feeling that touching food can cause them to gain weight at times. Often mothers with eating disorders find food mess difficult to cope with. The 1-year-old with the bent plastic spoon, using his or her pureed lunch as a percussion instrument, can cause particular challenges for the eating disordered mother who may sometimes take the spoon herself to feed the baby neatly, and wipe up any stray morsels of food that appear in the vicinity. This indicates that assessment of the mother/child relationship, especially around food and feeding is very important, and that adequate therapy and support needs to be provided as will be discussed later in this chapter.

## Patients in Hospital

Admission to an eating disorders unit can prove to be a major respite for a family attempting to support a seriously ill person with Anorexia Nervosa. The unit takes over the responsibility for meal provision and supervision and attempted prevention of self-destructive behaviours, everything that the family, whether parents or partner, has been attempting to achieve prior to admission. Some parents, understandably, immediately take a holiday. Communication in the age of the mobile does not cease and calls may continue to arrive, sometimes several times a day. They may be simple distress calls or 'get me out of here' demands. The latter can be very difficult to resist, particularly if the weight-gaining treatment is leading to extreme distress on the patient's part. The staff need to reassure the family about the role of inpatient care and the need for improved nutrition if the patient is to survive. Sometimes relatives rendered anxious and distressed by calls from the patient may phone the inpatient unit in order to transmit messages about clinical care. If this occurs frequently, it is useful to see the relative alone for a discussion, and to establish a route, generally via one specified team member, for concerns to be relayed to the team. In addition, it can be useful for the patient and her relatives to meet with the team often, as part of a regular team meeting to clarify lines of communication and address any outstanding concerns.

In the case of a patient with SEED, the aims of treatment may be very different from those admitted during the first few years of an eating disorder when restoration to near normal or normal BMI may be the aim to achieve before discharge. In someone who has maintained a BMI of say, 14, for a number of years, but who has as a result of a distressing event or an illness, lost weight to a BMI of 12, the aim of inpatient care may be to achieve weight restoration up to a level of BMI of 14 and no more. Preferably, if the inpatient team and the outpatient team are different, the patient and the family will all agree on the aims so that tension between the elements of the system can be avoided.

Prior to discharge to day or outpatient care, it is very important that relatives who may be accepting some responsibility are involved in discharge planning meetings, and that the primary care physician (general practitioner) is informed about the date of discharge in writing, and what is expected of the primary care team following discharge.

## Separated and Divorced Parents

At least half the patients will have parents living separately, sometimes in other relationships, and this can complicate therapy. Not infrequently, there are unresolved issues between the parents regarding abandonment, finances and other areas, and if they are to be seen together to discuss their offspring's difficulties, a truce on these issues need to be agreed. If that is not possible, it may be better for the parents to be seen separately, as disagreements over the care of the patient may become intertwined with the couple's disagreements and resentments. In this situation, decisions and policies agreed may need to be written and circulated by one of the team members to all involved. Quite commonly, however, parents whose sexual relationships has broken down, may be able to act in their parental role and come together to discuss issues without allowing their own difficulties to take over the field. Involving parents' new partners is a decision usually best left to the patient, and will depend on how much she feels accepted by the step-parent, and how much she can accept a new partner in her own parent's life.

# Siblings

Having a sibling with a chronic eating disorder almost always has a major impact on brothers and sisters. Some siblings distance themselves from the family, most of the attention having been provided to the patient. They may find alternative parental figures, may have relationships at a younger than average age and make major attempts to avoid involvement in the care of the patient, e.g. by moving to a distant part of the country or indeed another country. This can work reasonably well, although it carries with it a number of negative outcomes. Relationship with the patient is more or less lost, that with the parents can become critical and hostile while, not least in importance, the sibling him- or herself can feel guilty and remorseful.

Another rather extreme reaction is for the sibling to develop worrying symptoms or behaviour him- or herself. This can be an eating disorder, but might be drug abuse, self-harm or premature sexual activity. It is not necessarily the case that the symptom is a response to the sibling's eating disorder. It may have similar aetiological antecedents to the eating disorder in the index sibling. However, it certainly changes the balance in the family system, as parents then have two children with psychological problems, one with a long-term eating disorder and one with other psychiatric difficulties.

Siblings are often forgotten sufferers from psychiatric disorder in a family. Parents, especially mothers, gain the status of carer, the patient is the sufferer, the service user or the client, while siblings may have to share whatever attention is going with someone who requires a lot of care and who may repeatedly enter crises which may swamp the resources of the family. In spite of this, expressions of resentment by siblings are not often welcome, and may be seen as another burden for the family. As a result, many siblings distance themselves from the family, and obtain their support from friendships and relationships. This process occurs in any family in which one of the children is especially needy, whether from psychiatric or physical illness, and parents' attempts to cover all the needs of all the parties can leave them very thinly stretched. Sometimes recruiting uncles, aunts and grandparents can fill the gaps, although the siblings themselves may strongly resist any offers of support that might threaten their independence.

# Types of Approach to Family Issues

## *Whole (conjoint) family therapy*

In this model, the most familiar one, the patient is seen together with the rest of the family, usually those living together. However, siblings long gone from the household can join in, and if the patient is cohabiting the session can be in couple therapy. Family therapy has a mixed reputation amongst families, some finding the process very useful and others finding it highly unpleasant and blaming. Some of the negative consequences may arise from families' pre-existing beliefs that they are the cause of the eating disorder. Parents rightly believe that their behaviour influences their offspring's development. The influence of psychoanalysis in positing childhood experiences as key factors in the development of mental disorders has also contributed. Family therapy theory itself has led to therapists adopting a position which places family structure and function as major causative factors in eating disorders. The patient is often seen as behaving in a way that is helpful to the family, the anorexia drawing the attention of the parents towards the sick child and away from their own marital problems. Sometimes, the patient is seen as looking after one of the parents, usually the mother, to protect her from a marital relationship which might be violent, neglectful or simply out of steam.

While such dynamics may indeed be going on, it is not justified to posit them as causing the eating disorder and most family therapists now make efforts to avoid conveying this interpretation. More pragmatic approaches place the parents as essential agents in helping their son or daughter with the Anorexia Nervosa, and in shorter illnesses there is some evidence for the efficacy of this approach (Russell *et al.*, 1987). In long-term Anorexia Nervosa in which the aims of therapy usually include symptom minimization rather than cure, the family approach may be very different.

### *Patient V*

*A 20-year-old patient with Anorexia Nervosa since age 10 is living with her parents. She was treated in an inpatient unit in which discharge at the age of 14 was only allowed if the mother supervised each meal. She did so and the patient maintained her weight until the age of 20. At the mother's request, the family entered therapy together with the father and sister. While it was clear that the mother's efforts had ensured that her daughter had maintained a weight which allowed her to attain a normal adult height, as well as secondary sexual characteristics, she remained vulnerable. She was usually unable to eat without her mother's presence, and there seemed little prospect of her becoming independent from her mother. In family therapy, it was decided that at the patient's age it was appropriate to encourage her strongly to take some responsibility for eating. Accordingly, meals were left out that she was expected to manage to eat by herself. Over the next few weeks her weight fell and her BMI declined from 18 to 16. However, at that point her weight stabilized and further meal supervision was withdrawn. At the time, she was attending a day centre where her midday meal was provided. By the end of the exercise, her mother was not involved in meal supervision and she maintained a BMI of around 14. The following year she went abroad for a youth programme and her BMI remained low but stable.*

This case illustrates that as children enter the adult age range, it may be appropriate for them to begin to take responsibility for fulfilling their dietary requirements. This policy may not suit all families, and some may elect to continue intensive supervision indefinitely. It needs to be made explicit, however, that the general welfare of the family, including that of other siblings, may be compromised because of the emphasis on one family member. The decision for the family is difficult. At some point, the role of the family can change so that when intensive help is required it comes from psychiatric, medical and eating disorder services rather than the parents. This reflects developmental progression from childhood to adulthood and the process can be seen in many conditions, including for example, diabetes mellitus and cystic fibrosis, in which the parents' role changes from active provider of treatment (such as physiotherapy in cystic fibrosis) to supportive relative with active treatment being provided by visits to a clinic, or, perhaps by a close friend or partner. As in the case described above, the family may have to come to terms with the possibility that, without their intensive support, their son/daughter's health may decline to a new level, and this can be very hard to bear. Support from health care professionals, relatives and particularly, other parents, can be crucial.

### Subsets of families or other groupings

While family therapists in the past sometimes insisted that all family members be present at the session and refused to see a family that had travelled many miles, because of the absence of an expected member, most are now more pragmatic and less autocratic. This relaxation has led to creative opportunities to work on specific aspects of family relationships such as mother–daughter, father–daughter and sibling. The mother's role may dominate family therapy, as she is the one who takes most responsibility for provision of food, and fathers and siblings can be left out. This can be addressed within whole family therapy, but sessions with the different pairs in the family can be helpful and informative. When the patient has been suffering from the eating disorder for many years, the role of the family may be to help detect relapse, but often it is to learn to accept that one member of the family has a serious mental and physical disorder which is rather unlikely to recover, and to find ways of integrating that person so that she does not feel so much that she is an oddity and a failure in a family that she may see functioning successfully. When the patient is seen together with one other member, her contribution within that relationship may be more apparent, while the relative salience of the eating disorder can diminish. Thus, two sisters are seen together. One has had Anorexia Nervosa for 12 years, the other seems OK, but in the session, expresses her profound lack of confidence in dealing with sexual relationships. The 'patient' has had several boyfriends, and is able to advise her sister on this aspect of her life. Another patient with long-term Anorexia Nervosa is extremely close to her mother, and hardly relates to her father, who has distanced himself from both his daughter and his wife. A session with the father and daughter allows them to rediscover the lost appreciation that they have a similar sense of humour. Lastly, a pair of identical twins both develop Anorexia Nervosa which enters the chronic phase, becoming SEED. Their attachment to both mother and father is weakened by addiction and eating disorder in the parents, and they rely absolutely on each other for support. In therapy, one of them recovers her weight and gets on with her career, after 16 years of illness. They are then both faced with a terrible dilemma. If the second twin recovers, they may be forced to separate because of their divergent career paths. If one stays ill, the other will always need to be around to monitor her health and nurture her, being nurtured herself in return. Sessions for the twins help them appreciate this and, if the second twin is unable to recover, face the very difficult issues around separation for this vulnerable pair.

Individuals other than relatives can also be invited to sessions, including friends, godparents and even work colleagues. Care must be taken, however, that we do not collude with what may be an unhealthy process. Sometimes a work colleague, who may be a manager, may have developed rescue fantasies, perhaps reflecting conflicts over their role in relation to their own sick mother or sister for example. In a session, such issues may become apparent, but we do not always have permission to explore psychologically relevant issues with people other than patients and relatives. It is, in fact, arguable whether we have permission to do so with relatives who are not referred patients, but we do so, and take their arrival at our place of work as implying consent on the part of the patient. A friend or work colleague would need to give clear consent to being asked about sensitive areas, and might be willing to do so. Sometimes they are found to have problems with food, if not a major eating disorder, or other family issues that underlie their interest in helping their colleague, but not always, and their involvement can simply arise from concern for a sick co-worker, who may be far from family and so dealing with their problems alone. Friends can also provide helpful support and can be seen together with the patient. Someone with SEED often has developed close relationships, perhaps during treatment, with another person with an eating disorder and it may be appropriate to see them together. The dangers are: being drawn into providing treatment for the friend, which should be sought independently, and conversely, being concerned that the friend's symptoms (such as undereating, bingeing, etc.) might be adversely affecting the patient. These issues do need to be discussed if the two are seen together, and permission should be sought to contact the friend's therapist. Keeping boundaries clear can, however, be quite difficult in this situation.

## Multi-family groups

Services in which several families are seen together have been well documented (Robinson, 2006a; Colahan and Robinson, 2002; Dare and Eisler, 2000; Asen and Schmidt, 2005). There has not been a particular emphasis on patients with chronic eating disorders, although extrapolating from single family work can give us some guidance on how to manage such groups. Unlike the case in young patients with early onset of Anorexia Nervosa, in which the emphasis is on the parents encouraging the patient to eat and relinquish the anorexic lifestyle, the underlying aims of treatment will be quite different. For example, acceptance of certain behaviours as part of the patient's current way of being, living with anorexia or bulimia rather than getting rid of them and addressing difficulties in relationships which may be causing more stress when trying to live with the problem might well be the most helpful. For patients living separately from the family, issues will include managing phone calls, visits and meals out.

Different units have different ways of providing this approach. At the Russell Unit our approach to multi-family group workshops has been described in Colahan and Robinson (2002) and Robinson (2006a). We have also engaged in multi-couple workshops and in those we adopted a similar format, with sessions introducing the partner, 'goldfish bowl' discussions (in which the group is split and one sub-group, say, the females, talk while the males watch, or vice versa), art therapy, movement therapy, family sculpts, meals with staff and homework. These approaches have yet to be evaluated using controlled studies, and are at present in the realms of interesting approaches.

## *Family support*

Various forms of family support can be provided, including seeing relatives in outpatient sessions, including them in Care Programme Approach meetings, running regular groups for carers and organizing workshops and skills training for carers. In addition, organizations such as B-EAT in the United Kingdom (www.b-eat.co.uk) offer information and support to relatives of patients with eating disorders. There is a substantial rate of psychiatric disturbance in the carers of people with eating disorders (National Collaborating Centre for Mental Health, 2004), and in cases of severe long-term eating disorders the stress on relatives may be increased because of the unrelenting nature of the problems. An assessment of carers' needs can be offered under the Care Programme Approach and this should be discussed, even though many carers may prefer not to have an assessment of their needs. Confidentiality is often cited as a reason not to speak to relatives. However, an approach by the relative of an adult patient with an eating disorder need not be followed by disclosure of information about the patient. Questions such as 'How do I react if she spends all night exercising in her room?' can be addressed by using only information provided by the carer, so that no breach of confidentiality has occurred. Questions can also be addressed in general terms. It is intolerable to leave relatives of a patient with a potentially fatal disorder in ignorance of how to manage, especially if the patient is living in the same house.

# 6

# Care Programming in SEED

Following the Care Programme Approach (CPA), assessment of the patient with SEED needs to take into account the widest possible range of areas of difficulty, indicate what these difficulties are, the responses proposed and the person responsible for implementing the responses. In addition, the CPA meeting's agenda should include an anticipation of relapse and how services should respond if relapse occurs. At the meeting, it should be defined what the level of risk is, how it should be managed, and how family and carers should be involved, informed and supported. Lastly, it is important to decide on a date, time and place for the next meeting and who is responsible for convening it.

## Invitees

One member of the clinical team, the care coordinator, is responsible for inviting those attending. Those who actually attend will depend at least in part on the location and timing of the meeting. However, even if an individual is unable to attend, the invitation may trigger useful conversations with the patient and professionals before the meeting, which can be relayed to those attending. Those who should be considered for invitation are (1) the patient, (2) the care coordinator, (3) a relative, carer of friend chosen by the patient, (4) a representative from the general adult psychiatry service, (5) a representative from the eating disorders service, (6) an advocate, (7) an interpreter, (8) a representative from the service from which the patient

*Severe and Enduring Eating Disorder*   Paul Robinson
© 2009 John Wiley & Sons, Ltd

is being transferred, (9) representatives from services to which the patient is being transferred, (10) the GP and (11) any other relevant professional.

In practice, the attendance of the CPA meetings is somewhat weaker than ideal. For a GP, attendance at all the CPA meetings for a practice is not feasible and if the presence of the GP is essential, for example in the case of someone with somatization disorder with multiple medical consultations, then the meetings should be held in the General Practice if space allows.

Certain attendees are essential. If for example a patient is being transferred from an inpatient setting to a community mental health team, the attendance of members of the CMHT as well as an expert in eating disorders is essential; the latter, to assess and convey the degree of risk presented by the patient (Treasure, Schmidt and Hugo, 2005).

Some patients request or require a mental health advocate to be present if they feel intimidated by the proceedings or for other reasons wish to have an independent person in the room, while others request that a solicitor be present at a CPA meeting, sometimes at other gatherings such as team meetings. One patient for whom the author was the consultant, insisted on the presence of her solicitor and mental health advocate as well as a prominent politician who happened to be a family friend, making the CPA meeting large and potentially unruly.

## Issues Discussed in the Meeting

Each of the professionals will have a view about how the meeting should go. The meetings are generally collegial and friendly. The chair can be the care coordinator or one of the senior professionals present. The role of the chair is to introduce each person, make sure the patient and any relatives, carers or friends as well as professionals are at ease, and to explain the purpose of the meeting and how it will be conducted. Chairs differ in their view of how to structure the discussion, but an agenda which is often used is presented in Table 6.1, this will be used as a structure in the discussion that follows.

## Agenda for Care Programme Approach Meeting (see Table 6.1)

Introductions and apologies
Explanation about the meeting, the CPA process and the form

**Table 6.1** Suggested agenda for a CPA meeting

Agenda for a CPA meeting
    1. Invitees, present and apologies
    2. Introductions and explanations
    3. Identification of care coordinator
    4. Domains
        a. Mental health problems
        b. Medical problems
        c. Occupational issues
        d. Financial issues
        e. Accommodation
        f. Families and carers
        g. Other issues, e.g. legal
    5. Risk assessment
    6. Relapse indicators
    7. Date, time and place of next meeting

*Mental health problems*

This can include a statement about eating and weight disorder, any personality problems and any additional psychiatric problems such as depression, obsessional and compulsive disorder and deliberate self-harm. This part can be potentially distressing for a patient whose list of problems sound to her like a catalogue of failings, and it may be useful to refer to areas in relatively vague non-technical terms such as 'difficulties with food', poor nutrition, low mood, etc. The formal diagnoses may or may not appear on the form depending on the wishes of a patient, although they should always have been discussed with the patient prior to the meeting.

It is also extremely important that the chair has met with the patient beforehand to check what may be discussed in the meeting. For example, cocaine abuse is not uncommon in patients with long-standing eating disorders and the CPA meeting may not be the most helpful situation in which a parent first learns about it. Any sensitive issue such as sexual abuse should normally not be referenced although a patient with; for example, post-traumatic stress disorder might be agreeable to such a history being labelled 'childhood trauma'. A good deal of sensitivity is required of the chair who needs to make sure the meeting does what it is supposed to do, namely establish a care plan for someone without avoiding discussion of what is necessary and relevant but not expose the patient to a humiliating public exposé which can serve as a traumatic event in itself. The CPA meeting is not a 'ward round' or an examination of the patient's history or mental state. It is, at least in part, a meeting to point to services that must be made available to the patient and her family and carers, if humanly possible, and to name health care professionals responsible for the delivery of those services.

Discussion of psychiatric problems must, therefore, include an indication of what the services intend to do about them. Thus, for the eating disorder in the patient with SEED intervention may include physical monitoring, outpatient support, referral to a self-help group and dietetic advice. Plans should be made about what to do if weight falls or other parameters indicating risk such as serum potassium or ECG results pass danger thresholds.

Interventions can range from more frequent attendance at a clinic or at the GP, or prescription of dietary supplements or potassium tablets. If the risk is higher, referral to A&E (accident and emergency department) or admission to a medical or eating disorders bed might be considered. These latter options can form part of the planned response to relapse mentioned below.

Patients with SEED have often had a good deal of therapy and many respond to the notion of more psychotherapy with scepticism. Specific therapies such as cognitive behaviour therapy or psychoanalytic treatment should perhaps be reserved for other identifiable problems, and can be time limited. The precise model of therapy (CPT, analytic, etc.) is probably of less importance than the provision of a safe environment in which to explore thoughts, feelings and behaviours which relate to the problem. For example, a patient with long-term Anorexia Nervosa (restricting type) who for the first time develops bulimic symptoms may respond to a series of sessions focused on dealing with and avoiding bingeing and controlling vomiting, laxative abuse and restriction. A patient with stable SEED complicated by deliberate self-harm and other features of borderline personality disorder may respond to therapy such as dialectical behaviour therapy or mentalization-based therapy aimed at reducing self-harming behaviours. In general, however, the psychological help offered to a patient who has run the gamut of available therapies and who may be requesting a 'therapy holiday' can reasonably be confined to support and monitoring.

## Medication

When psychological approaches have failed to bring about permanent improvement and the patient is left with SEED, clinicians often turn to medication to alleviate the misery in which the patient remains. In spite of the fact that there is little evidence of the effectiveness of any psychotropic medication – antidepressants, mood stabilizers or anti-psychotic drugs – they are all prescribed and patients with sleeplessness due to low weight may be given sedative antidepressants such as Mirtazapine or anti-psychotic drugs such as Olanzapine. As long as the patient is not risking permanent damage such as can occur with long-term anti-psychotic medication, the use of antidepressants to treat insomnia and anxiety and perhaps depression may be helpful. The plethora of drugs that many patients with eating disorders find themselves taking are eloquent testimony to the sad fact that we have no effective drug treatment for Anorexia Nervosa. The use of antidepressants in bulimia nervosa uncomplicated by severe malnutrition has a reasonable evidence base. Almost every antidepressant has been tried in bulimia in what seemed to be a headlong race funded by the pharma industry which was eventually won by Prozac, although the majority of antidepressants tested did suppress bingeing to some extent. There is very little information on long-term effects of medication and, in particular, whether the gains of medication outlive its discontinuation. Given the problems coming off SSRI's especially at the high doses used in bulimia nervosa, it is very surprising that NICE chose to recommend antidepressants as an alternative to an evidence-based self-help course for patients with bulimia nervosa (National Collaborating Centre for Mental Health, 2004).

## Medical problems

Patients with eating disorders, especially those with SEED, have a wide range of medical problems most of them the effects of starvation or purging. Management can often not eliminate or reverse the damage but must alleviate and improve function as far as possible to optimize quality of life in a chronic disease. Thus, osteoporosis can be managed with bone mineral density scans at 1 to 2 year intervals and treated sensibly but without an evidence base with calcium and vitamin D and possibly with hormone replacement therapy or an oral contraceptive. The use of biphosphonates is controversial as already indicated in the discussion of the treatment of osteoporosis in Anorexia Nervosa in Chapter 3.

Potassium chloride (Slow K, Sando K) may be given for hypokalaemia and medical monitoring including body mass index, SUSS test, U and E, full blood count and liver function tests and ECG can be offered for those at risk.

Gastroenterology consultation is useful for patients with oesophagitis or peptic ulcer disease and to exclude significant organic pathology in patients with non-specific abdominal symptoms who are usually thought to have irritable bowel syndrome. Referral to a specialist in osteoporosis is indicated for patients unable to gain weight who may be candidates for biphosphonates.


## Occupational issues

Some patients with chronic eating disorders are able to find work which provides structured daytime activity. However, for the rest, filling time may be a real problem and the help of an occupational therapist can be invaluable. As described in Chapter 4, structured social and occupational activity sometimes competes with eating disorder related symptoms such as bingeing, buying, preparing and eating food, chewing and spitting, and obsessional and ritualistic behaviour such as cleaning. Indeed, the patient might be quite reluctant to give up these activities which may take several hours each day and replace them with, say, voluntary employment in a school or charity. Some patients can embark on educational activities and can be put in touch with educational establishments and listings of courses.

For both groups, those with and without work, social life can be a desert and advice on social activities including Internet chat rooms and eating disorder self-help groups can be useful.


## Financial issues

As noted, some patients have trouble spending (see Chapter 4) and may need help in, for example, fitting out a flat. Others may lose control on finances or overspend on food, alcohol or drugs and get into financial trouble needing help from a member of the multi-disciplinary team. Many patients are reluctant to apply for state benefits and can be encouraged to do so and helped to fill in the forms. For medical report writers, it may not always be clear that a patient has need of, say, a free travel pass. However, if the inner compulsion to walk off meals is coupled with difficulty spending and low weight, it is not surprising that many patients who should be using public transport do not and this (combined with a refused driving license) can form the basis for a request for a travel pass.

## Accommodation

This may well be an important issue in a patient who is struggling to become independent by leaving home but is unable to find alternative accommodation. Local authorities often run a points system and public housing is allocated first to people with more medical points. Patients may have a tendency to minimize their problems, sometimes due to low self-esteem or ambivalence about leaving home and encouragement to describe difficulties with precision, supported by a carefully worded medical report with details of the patient's disabilities can increase the likelihood of successful re-housing being achieved.

## Families and carers

The role of the family has been discussed in Chapter 5. If a family member is present, questions regarding support and information for the family and family therapy and support can be part of the care plan. If there is significant burden on the family (or if the family request it), they can receive a separate carers assessment which can feed into the CPA process.

## Other issues, for example legal

Any other problems not hitherto covered can be addressed. The patient may have legal problems relating to shop lifting or stealing money and may require help in dealing with this. Issues relating to the Mental Health and Capacity Acts can be dealt with here. The patient may be treated on a community order and have to comply with certain requirements, or a very messy and untidy home with food around or stored can evince the interest of environmental health departments especially if rodents are in evidence.

*Risk assessment*

A written assessment of risk has become essential in the record of a patient with mental health problems. Many senior health care professionals have adopted an optimistic approach to new regulation about risk, tinged with a variable proportion of paranoia and cynicism. Paranoid cynics among health care professionals assert that the forms are there to know who to blame when things go wrong. Naive optimists assert that careful risk assessment is a valuable and clinically beneficial part of the overall assessment, and should be welcomed as long as it does not become a form filling exercise in which everyone we see has to have a formal risk assessment. Forms for such an assessment may not suit patients with eating disorders that well, as they are usually designed to record risk of suicide, self-neglect or homicide. Nutrition rarely appears, and we need to tick the box labelled Severe Self Neglect as the idea that seems closest to self-starvation from the list. Given that risk assessment is such a major part of management of eating disorders, we should, perhaps have our own risk assessment form, including an online version for computerized systems, which are spreading rapidly. A suggested set of questions is presented in Table 6.2. Apart from nutrition, electrolyte and fluid imbalance, renal, cardiac and liver function, as well as potential for suicide and lesser forms of self-harm, should all be represented. 'Harm to others' rarely seems relevant, unless relatives' (and clinicians') sleepless nights and panic attacks are counted.

*Relapse indicators*

This section can sometime seem rather gloomy as if the team is predicting that the patient's health will fail. However, it is important to indicate to all present what might go wrong. The important question is 'What should

**Table 6.2** Risk in eating disorders

| |
| --- |
| Items for a risk assessment form for use in eating disorders |
| 1. Risk due to inadequate nutritional intake |
| 2. Risk due to vomiting |
| 3. Risk due to abuse of laxatives or other medications |

trigger increased intensity of treatment?' The most common trigger is significant change in the results of medical monitoring and this may be a change in weight, muscle power, blood tests such as potassium or ECG. Secondly, the trigger might be changes in mental state indicating an increased risk of self-harm. The triggers should each be accompanied by a general statement about what the responsive services might be, examples include increased monitoring, day care, home visits, hospital admission and family involvement. A trigger might be discontinuing medical monitoring visits when weight or other risk factors are worrying. The action on the part of the key worker, agreed in advance by the patient at the CPA meeting, may be to contact the GP or family, arrange a visit at the GP or to arrange a home visit.

## Next meeting

This is very often left blank but should always be filled in, if only to ensure reappearance of those present at the meeting. It is useful to prepare in advance a number of potential dates with the same time and place as the present meeting, an appropriate time ahead which usually extends between 3 and 6 months depending on how rapidly things seem to be changing.

## CPA in action

### Patient S

*The Teetering Coper*

*Patient S is a 45-year-old woman with restricting Anorexia Nervosa, which began when she was 16. At initial assessment, her physical state was quite poor with a BMI of 12.9, inability to rise easily from squatting (scored 2 out of 3 on SUSS) or to sit up from lying flat (score 1 out of 3). There is mild elevation in her liver enzymes. However, her energy levels were good and she held down a highly responsible job as the production manager for a prestigious scientific journal. Her parents were alive but her mother was rather frail, and they lived some 50 miles away. She herself lived in her own flat and had no particular accommodation or financial problems.*

*Assessment*

At the CPA meeting the following conclusions were reached: psychiatric problems, severe Anorexia Nervosa restricting sub-type with critically low weight. No other psychiatric disorder:

1. *Intervention.* Weekly monitoring at the GP, 6 weekly appointments with eating disorders consultant.
2. *Medical.* Problem: raised liver enzymes (anorexic hepatitis), muscle weakness. Management: regular weekly blood tests to include LFTs, creatine kinase, electrocardiogram and SUSS.
3. *Occupational.* No identified issues.
4. *Financial.* No identified issues.
5. *Accommodation.* No identified issues.
6. *Family.* Offer appointment for parents to be seen with their daughter. Inform about self-help services for families.
7. *Relapse indicators.* Parameters: falling weight, increasing liver function tests, weakness, cardiac abnormalities. Triggers: two consecutive losses of weight, two consecutive increases of liver function tests, negative change in SUSS score, any ECG abnormality. Action: (a) urgent medical review; (b) weekly monitoring at eating disorders unit; (c) consider increasing intensity of treatment (medical admission, eating disorders admission) if no improvement.

*Progress*

Over the next 3 months, the patient did well maintaining her weight and all the parameters stayed within acceptable limits. However, her mother was then diagnosed with metastatic cancer of the breast. Patient S took time off to help her father nurse her mother who died only 3 months later. She had been particularly close to her mother and was grief-stricken at her death. Her father, needing support himself moved in with her and she found herself doing far more domestic activities than before.

Weekly physical assessment revealed a marked fall in weight to BMI 12.1 and her muscle power declined (SUSS test sit-up 0 out of 3, squat-stand 1 out of 3). Her liver enzymes increased slightly but remained less than 100. Other tests were normal. She was interviewed by the consultant psychiatrist and told that unless she could turn her weight loss around, admission was inevitable. She very much wanted to avoid inpatient care and at her next assessment 3 days later her BMI was 12.4 and 4 days after that 12.8. Her liver enzymes fell back to normal. Much to her relief she avoided hospital admission and was able to remain at home to support her father while her outpatient physical monitoring continued.

### Patient L

*It's my stomach!*

*This 26-year-old suffered from Anorexia Nervosa since the age of 14 when she began vomiting, then bingeing and vomiting after meals. Her mother was clinically ill and underweight due to inflammatory bowel disease, and the patient witnessed frequent life-threatening crises in her mother. From an early stage in her illness, she complained of abdominal pains, constipation and diarrhoea and she was diagnosed as suffering from irritable bowel syndrome. Her weight was low, BMI 16 and at the age of 18 she was referred to the eating disorders services for assessment and treatment receiving outpatient, day patient and inpatient treatment as well as individual, group and family therapy although her mother rarely attended the latter because of irritable bowel disease crises. During outpatient follow-up, she gradually gained weight but at a BMI of 17.5 she broke off attendance and saw a gastroenterologist for treatment of her IBS. During the following 6 months, she lost a large amount of weight ending up with a BMI of only 14. Since then her BMI has remained between 12 and 14, and 12 years after the onset she remains very severely anorexic with continuing symptoms of bowel disturbance.*

Her management plan was as follows:

1. *Psychiatric.* She has been offered weekly medical monitoring, BMI, SUSS, U and E, LFTs, CK and ECG. Regarding additional therapy, she argues that she has already had years of individual psychotherapy; she feels she has covered the most relevant issues and prefers to follow her life activities without worrying about therapy appointments.
2. *Medical.* Her gastroenterology consultations have led to serious crises in her health and can be seen as an avoidance behaviour. Hence, active communication between the psychiatrist and the gastroenterology teams is essential. The agreement reached was for the psychiatrist to discuss care with the gastroenterologist or at least to send an email prior to each appointment with either.

3. *Occupation.* The patient is pursuing a university course. No identified issues.
4. *Finances.* No identified issues.
5. *Accommodation.* The patient lives in her own flat, sometimes staying with her parents and no current issues were identified.
6. *Family.* The family have access to parental sessions and the carers support group.

*Relapse indicators.* These are largely nutritional with weight loss, SUSS, U and E, hyponatraemia (due to water loading), hypokalaemia (due to vomiting), liver function tests and creatine kinase being the main indicators. In cold weather, her core body temperature is measured and hypothermia would result in a diagnosis of relapse. Any indication of relapse would trigger an urgent medical assessment.

# A Pilot Case Series Using Qualitative and Quantitative Methods: Biological, Psychological and Social Outcome in Severe and Enduring Eating Disorder (Anorexia Nervosa)[1]

James Arkell[1] and Paul Robinson

[1] *Department of Mental Health Sciences, Royal Free and University College Medical School, London, UK*

Anorexia Nervosa is a psychiatric disorder characterized by refusal of an individual to maintain a minimum normal body weight, often to the point of starvation. The core feature is an intense fear of gaining weight (World Health Organization, 1992; American Psychiatric Association 1994). It affects primarily young women. There has been a small increase in the global incidence of this illness throughout the twentieth century, but in the United Kingdom over the past 12 years the incidence has been remarkably stable for women aged 10–39 at about 20 per 100 000 (Currin *et al.*, 2005). The peak age at onset of Anorexia Nervosa is the mid-teens and that of bulimia nervosa is 2 or 3 years later. The average duration of Anorexia Nervosa is 6 years (Treasure, Schmidt and Hugo, 2005). However, up to 20% of patients presenting with Anorexia Nervosa have gone on to develop a severely disabling chronic form of the illness, SEED-AN (Robinson, 2006b), with significant physical, psychological and social disability. There are often significant co-morbidities such as depression, anxiety, obsessive compulsive

---

[1] Paper reprinted with permission from the International Journal of Eating Disorders, 2008. Wiley Interscience.

---

*Severe and Enduring Eating Disorder*    Paul Robinson
© 2009 John Wiley & Sons, Ltd

disorder and personality disorder (Sullivan *et al.*, 1998; Steinhausen, 2002). There is a long-term mortality rate of about 5% (Steinhausen, 2002), although some studies have shown it to be as high as 15% (Ratnasuriya *et al.*, 1991; Theander, 1985; Crisp *et al.*, 1992). Most studies have reported on cohorts and have not reported in detail, exclusively on patients with the severe chronic form of Anorexia Nervosa. Moreover, the National Institute of Clinical Excellence Guidelines for Eating Disorders (National Collaborating Centre for Mental Health, 2004) do not make provision for the specific needs of this sub-group of patients. Studies assessing quality of life in eating disorders have focused mainly on participants in the acute phase of the illness (Abraham *et al.*, 2006).

The level of impairment has been benchmarked against the healthy (Mond *et al.*, 2005; de la Rie *et al.*, 2006) or the physically ill (Keilen *et al.*, 1994) participants, rather than those with other mental illness.

There are established tools to measure disability in chronic mental illness (Rosen, Hadzi-Pavlovic and Parker, 1989; Parker *et al.*, 1991), but they have been rarely used in the context of eating disorders. This study aims to assess in detail the level of disability and quality of life in participants who have been consistently ill with Anorexia Nervosa for over 10 years. It aims to benchmark the level of impairment in both these domains against standardized samples with severe mental illness. This study will examine the proposition that Anorexia Nervosa in a chronic form is a serious psychiatric disorder that leads to a global impairment of functioning similar to that of schizophrenia.

# Method

## *Participants and recruitment*

All the participants were known to the The Russell Unit Eating Disorders Service. This is a community-focused service in North London, which at the time of the study covered a population of approximately 750 000. All participants were between 18 and 60 years old. An activity sheet of all outpatient contacts for one month at the unit was assembled. A total of 27 participants with a greater than 10-year history of a diagnosis of an eating disorder were identified through review of the case notes. (They must have continuously fulfilled the criteria for an ICD-10 (World Health Organization, 1992) diagnosis of Anorexia Nervosa F50.0 apart from temporary (<3 months) weight restoration due to hospital admission).

Of these 27 participants, 5 were excluded due to either pregnancy or severe illness leading to either physical inability or lack of capacity to consent. The 22 remaining were contacted by mail or telephone and asked to attend the Russell Unit for a 1-hour interview. Three declined and eight did not respond. The remaining 11 attended the interview. The mean age was 37.7 years (sd = 8 years).

The mean BMI was 15.8 kg/m$^2$ (sd = 2 kg/m$^2$). There were 10 females and 1 male. All were in active treatment. Of the 16 not included in the study, BMI mean was 16.2 kg/m$^2$ (sd = 0.8 kg/m$^2$) and age mean was 31.9 years (sd = 6.4 years). Ethical approval for the study was obtained prior to starting the study.

### Quantitative measures and procedure

A combination of subjective and objective assessment tools were used. The interview included questions about past psychiatric treatments and physical health.

*Questionnaires Used   Beck depression inventory (BDI) (Beck, Steer and Brown, 1996).* The revised BDI is a 21-item self-assessment of depression severity. Total scores of 0–9 indicate no significant symptoms, 10–18 mild/moderate symptoms, 19–29 moderate/severe depression and 30–63 extremely severe depression.

*Maudsley obsessive compulsive inventory (MOCI) (Hodgson and Rachman, 1977).* This is a 30-item, true-false, self-report questionnaire containing statements regarding OCD symptoms. It is not a diagnostic scale. The original data showed obsessional patients to score an average of 18.86 (sd = 4.92) compared to non-obsessional neurotic patients scoring 9.27 (sd = 5.43).

*The eating disorders inventory (EDI) (Garner, Olmsted and Polivy, 1983).* This is a 64-item, self-report questionnaire, designed to provide information on eight separate dimensions of cognitive and behavioural aspects of Anorexia Nervosa and bulimia. The eight subscales that comprise the EDI are called: Drive for Thinness (DT), Bulimia (B), Body Dissatisfaction (BD), Ineffectiveness (I), Perfectionism (P), Interpersonal Distrust (ID), Interoceptive Awareness (IA), and Maturity Fears (MF). A maximum of 142 is possible. The anorexic group in the original study scored a mean of 89.4 and the female comparison group scored 32.

*Bulimic investigatory test, Edinburgh (BITE) (Henderson and Freeman, 1987).* This is a self-report questionnaire for the detection and description of binge eating. It has established satisfactory reliability and validity. The scale has measures of both symptoms and severity. A symptom score of 20 or more indicates highly disordered eating pattern and binge eating. A severity score indicates the frequency of bingeing and purging. A score of over 5 is clinically significant.

*Life skills profile (LSP) (Rosen, Hadzi-Pavlovic and Parker, 1989; Parker et al., 1991).* This is an objective questionnaire completed by the interviewer. It was developed as a measure of those aspects of functioning 'life skills' which affected how successfully people with schizophrenia lived in the community or in a hospital. However, the LSP has been applied to a broad range of diagnoses. The LSP rates functions on five domains and gives an overall total score. Self-care reflects an ability to attend to personal hygiene, financial, nutritional and medical needs. Responsibility reflects a willingness to cooperate with health services and to look after personal possessions. Social contact describes the degree to which the person can maintain friendships, demonstrate interpersonal warmth and participate in social groups. Communication describes an ability to converse appropriately and coherently. Non-turbulence includes reckless, offensive, aggressive and irresponsible behaviour including substance misuse and criminal behaviour.

*The World Health Organization quality of life assessment (WHOQOL-100) (Skevington, 1999; Skevington and Wright, 2001).* This is a multi-dimensional multi-lingual profile for subjective assessment. It is a generic measure de-signed for use with a wide spectrum of physical and psychological disorders. Hundred items are attached to a five-point Likert response scale and high scores (recoded for negatively framed items) denote high QOL. The UK instrument shows excellent psychometric qualities of internal consistency, reliability and construct validity. The maximum score for each domain is 20 with a maximum total score for the six domains of 120. The domains measured are physical, psychological, independence, social relations, environment and spiritual.


### Qualitative procedure

The participant was also invited to write for up to 10 minutes about their own understanding of the key factors that underpinned their quality of life. They were given a pro-forma with 'anorexia my friend' and 'anorexia my enemy' as subsections. A similar method has been used for eating disorders in previous studies (Serpell and Treasure, 2002; Serpell et al., 1999).

# Results

*(Correlation coefficients above 0.67 were statistically significant with p = 0.025).*

### BDI scores

The mean score for the 11 participants was 33.5 (sd = 12.7), which falls in the severely depressed range. There was a strong negative correlation between BDI scores and total LSP scores (−0.95). A significant negative correlation was found between BDI scores and the total scores for WHOQOL-100 (−0.78) and the psychological component (−0.85).

### MOCI scores

The mean score for participants was 13.7 (sd = 8.2). Three participants scored over 20. The MOCI scores correlated significantly with BDI (0.71) and EDI (0.72) scores. However, correlation with LSP was only just significant (−0.68) and not significant with WHOQOL-100 scores (−0.53).

### BITE scores

'Symptom' score mean was 13.4 (sd = 6.6) and 'severity' score mean was 3.4 (sd = 4.6). Only three participants scored over 20 on the symptom score and over 5 on the severity score. This indicates that only three participants had clinically significant bulimic symptoms. Correlations with BITE scores did not reach significance with either LSP (−0.58, −0.57) or with WHOQOL-100 Scores (−0.58, −0.51).

### EDI scores

The score mean was 80.8 (sd = 25.6). EDI scores did not significantly negatively correlate with LSP total scores (−0.64) or with WHOQOL-100 total scores (−0.65). EDI correlated very highly with the psychological scores on WHOQOL-100 (−0.90) probably partly because they both include questions about body image.

**Table 7.1** Comparison of LSP scores of participants with Anorexia Nervosa and a standardized community sample of participants with schizophrenia (Parker *et al.*, 1991)

| Life Skills Profile score domains | Maximum possible score | Standardized community sample (*N* = 128) | Participants with Anorexia Nervosa (*N* = 11) |
|---|---|---|---|
| | | Mean (sd) | Mean (sd) |
| Self-care | 40 | 31 (6.3) | 32.9 (4.7) |
| Non-turbulence | 48 | 39 (6.7) | 44.6 (4.7) |
| Social contact | 24 | 14 (3.9) | 17 (4.9) |
| Communication | 24 | 19 (3.3) | 23.7 (0.5) |
| Responsibility | 20 | 16 (3.3) | 19.8 (0.4) |
| Total score | 156 | 119 (117.7) | 136.4 (13.3) |

## LSP scores

The LSP scores were compared with those of a standardized community sample of patients with schizophrenia (Parker *et al.*, 1991). Unlike the patients with schizophrenia, the participants with Anorexia Nervosa scored highly on communication and responsibility. However, their scores for self-care, non-turbulence and social contact approached that of the community sample of patients with schizophrenia. There was a significant positive correlation between total WHOQOL-100 scores and LSP scores (0.75).

## WHOQOL scores

As a comparison group scores were taken from a study assessing quality of life in a community sample of 106 adult patients (mean age of 41.4 years, 74% women) visiting their GP for moderate to severe depression in the South East of England (Skevington and Wright, 2001). Participants with Anorexia Nervosa scored remarkably similarly on the WHOQOL-100 when compared to this primary care population with depression.

(The scores for depression in this group were slightly less than those for the participants with Anorexia Nervosa. The mean BDI score of 25.4 (11) indicating moderate/severe depression compared to 33.5 (12.7) for the participants with Anorexia Nervosa, which is in the extremely severely depressed category.)

**Table 7.2** Comparison of WHOQOL scores of participants with Anorexia Nervosa and scores in a primary care population with depression (Skevington and Wright, 2001).

| WHOQOL domains | WHOQOL scores | WHOQOL scores |
|---|---|---|
| | Participants with Anorexia Nervosa ($N = 11$) Mean (sd) | Primary care population with depression ($N = 106$) Mean |
| Physical health | 11.9 (2) | 11.0 |
| Psychological | 9.2 (2.3) | 9.9 |
| Level of independence | 13.3 (3.3) | 13.0 |
| Social relations | 10.4 (1.4) | 11.3 |
| Environment | 13.3 (2.4) | 12.7 |
| Spiritual | 9 (3.3) | 10.4 |
| Total | 67.1 (10.8) | 68.18 |

A significant negative correlation was found between BDI scores and the total scores for WHOQOL-100 ($-0.78$) and the psychological component of WHOQOL-100 showed an even stronger correlation to BDI ($-0.85$). It is unsurprising that mood and subjective perception of QOL is highly correlated as it was also in the primary care population.

It is interesting that BDI scores also correlated highly with EDI scores (0.73) making it difficult to unpick mood from eating disordered symptoms or conclude that mood alone accounts for the poor QOL scores.

BMI and BDI scores surprisingly did not correlate highly with the physical component of WHOQOL-100 (0.37, $-0.46$), where one would have anticipated that mood and body mass would have informed perception of physical health.

### Qualitative data and analysis

The data from the unstructured writing was explored using standard, recommended qualitative methods. Individual transcripts were read repeatedly by JA and through this process emerging common themes and ideas were identified. In qualitative analysis, the next step is the development of a thematic framework, which can be systematically applied to the data. The data would then be coded according to an index derived from this framework. A chart would then be developed onto which quotes could be sorted under each relevant theme. Once the data was charted it would be possible to identify the key characteristics and interpret the data set. The key themes emerging were that of interpersonal avoidance and avoidance of intrapersonal mood states. Other themes were self-punishment, self-denial, self-control, family and physical health.

## Positive Aspects of Eating Disorders

### Interpersonal avoidance

'Familiar/safe'; 'Reliable'; 'Avoids having to cope with life'; 'It's a way of knowing I have an automatic way of knowing/feeling I have something to run to'; 'Out of all friends I could have had I chose you. There was no obvious alternative perhaps because I didn't look. I come to you when I don't want to be seen'; 'You provide me with explanations like when I don't turn up or miss the occasion when I am too late. You dry my tears and hide my littleness from others. You save me from standing up for myself – from saying no'; 'I can trust it and rely on it because it is so strict, I know where I stand. In a way the anorexia can be a good excuse to keep me away from others. It can act as a get out clause, an excuse . . . . it ensures I don't get close or comfortable with anyone of anything and keeps me on guard'; 'It's the marriage or relationship I thought would come so easily with humans. It is always there for me stopping me feeling alone'; 'The amount of time being anorexic takes cuts off situations it would have been hard to face'; 'I don't need anyone else or have to interact with anyone else, I can manage without any interference from anyone.'

### Intrapersonal avoidance

'Avoids having to face feelings'; 'It gives me something to think about if I'm bored or awake in the early morning'; 'I couldn't cope without it. Life would be harder and I would be more depressed and my feelings would be strange and not blocked by tiredness or lack of food. I couldn't have a better life so it blocks some unpleasant feelings'; 'You close my eyes when I don't want to know and knock me out when I don't wish to feel'; 'It helps me cope with life and keeps me safe and safe from the badness in the world'; 'Keeps my demons locked away, of inadequacy, failure, weakness, indecision, reaching expectations, criticism, feeling vulnerable, exposed, angry, sad etc., easier to avoid situations where I feel those feelings. Life is less complicated, less fearful, less uncertain.'

## Control/restraint

'Ensures that I remain disciplined and in control. By keeping things strict it avoids ambiguity and generally there is a rule for everything so no decision is entirely based just on my wants and desires'; 'The anorexia ensures I don't become selfish or greedy, it lowers the chance of me losing control or overindulging'; 'If I wasn't anorexic I would be out of control'; 'Quite comforting knowing I'm never going to eat too much'; 'Allows me to feel secure about my eating habits.'

## Achievement/purpose

'Feel a sense of purpose, a drive'; 'Sense of achievement/superiority'; 'Challenges such as walking, exercising, restricting provide a sense of achievement, structure and routines. occupies my mind. Makes me feel strong and push myself to extremes, denying myself things. Fills an emptiness, void within myself. Creates my own world with rules, shoulds/shouldn'ts and the real world fades, matters less'; 'It gives me a structure to the day'; 'Feel tired at the end of the day'; 'Strength, because it requires discipline and acting on rules. Sense of achievement, because I am quite good at it'; 'Helps my depression because I feel I am looking after myself by letting me do/eat what I want a few times a week. Gives me something to look forward to something that is mine. Takes up time.'

## Self-punishment/self-denial

'By keeping control of me the anorexia prevents me from being to kind to myself, becoming selfish because If I was to start doing what I want I run the risk of not putting other people and their needs before mine, thus giving people more of a reason to dislike and hurt me'; 'When I hate myself it's a way to treat myself badly. It is like a self-destruct button and this has been what I wanted sometimes'; 'It's enabling me to get into clothes that I love, I eat cake and it doesn't put weight on me because if I have it because if I have I cut back on the rest of the meal. I'm not on any diets and eat anything I fancy – it's just I end up missing protein out or eating fruit and salads if I'm eating out later.'

## Negative Aspects of Eating Disorders

### *Interpersonal avoidance*

'I don't belong in the world. I'll never be good enough for your world and I most certainly don't belong in the real world, I just don't belong'; 'Social isolation'; 'Lies, manipulation to maintain habit'; 'It's made my social life a bit difficult – few of my friends that know me with eating problems ever invite me over for a meal. There are some friends who still make me really nervous and I sometimes can't eat at all around them or end up bursting into tears because they try to force me or tell me off and I feel dreadful'; 'I like people and it has isolated me because I can't go into most social situations easily. I don't like being single but I don't stand much chance of anything else'; 'Creates loneliness isolation. Difficult to do anything that breaks routines e.g. visit from family, friends, work, college course etc'; 'Difficult to feel comfortable around people and in situations. Brings peoples negative attention towards me'; 'Makes relationships almost impossible to make and maintain'; 'At first the anorexia just controlled food but over the years it has gradually seeped into all other aspects of my life taking my life away piece by piece. It has taken away and is controlling not only food but friends, family, career interests, self-worth. . .basically I went from having a life to have nothing but you in my life. You make me feel sad and depressed, worthless, useless and lonely'; 'Makes me feel unsociable, unable to eat with others. Makes me want to hide, a freak, inflexible, trapped'; 'Initially you seemed like a friend and although you keep me company and stop me from feeling alone you have managed to rid the few people whom I did have. The anorexia has taken me out of the "world" all alone and into its own world where there is no one but me'; 'It blocks some true feelings and relationships and I don't experience as much as I could'; 'I now think I don't have any close friends because they all got fed up with me'; 'I see life going on around me but feel distanced, displaced from it.'

## Impact on family

'I am deeply sorry that I have put my family though all sorts of worry and upset'; '"Real" world becomes more and more alien and difficult to remain in. Damages relationships with family and friends. Puts them in a situation where other people feel the need to take responsibility for my eating and health. Puts me in a situation where I need to be hospitalized'; 'It has caused a great deal of worry and pain to my family'; 'I wish my mother had not died with a memory of me like this. I have let down so many people who have tried to help.'

## Achievement/purpose

'It has ruined my life and changed it. When younger I used to burst out sometimes and feel really upset about my situation but I don't now. Is that as I feel better or is that part of me stifled and I cant see the illness as an illness/problem but normal for me now'; 'I haven't achieved as much as I should – I would like a PhD. I can't concentrate as much as I should be able to'; 'Activities become mindless rituals with no value or worth'; 'The anorexia has taken away all my confidence and self esteem. I'm never good enough. I'll never reach my best'; 'You're erasing my memory as well as my mind – suspending my aspirations, muddling my wishes and interfering with my spirit. You're sucking me out. You quash my dreams.'

'The hate sometimes is excruciating like a pain you want to leave, only this desire and control slots itself into every corner of my mind and I have allowed it to run parallel with my everyday life. THE CELL I HAVE BUILT FOR MYSELF!!' 'You get angry when I tell you and come back with a vengeance. When I cry and really need to, when I write and really want to. You stop me from believing – succeeding in mid-sentence'; 'Life less meaning, more wooden, no passion, joy, ups, downs. Everyday activities become a chore and irritant e.g. shaving showering, washing clothes.'

*Physical health/appearance*

'Sleeplessness'; 'Feel cold'; 'Can't sleep properly. Become irritable and an-
noyed and constantly "talk" in my head'; 'I cannot control my weight
loss below a certain weight and become ill'; 'I feel ashamed of being a
slave to something so crazy. I have many physical problems because of
chronic low weight. Although I don't see myself objectively I know I look
awful and that matters to me. I can't buy clothes easily'; 'Makes me feel
ill, thirsty, tired and anxious'; 'You make me frail and fragile. You make
me think too early that I'm too late. You provide me with sickness and a
strong reminder that I can't ever defend myself'; 'Out of touch with reality
(without knowing it).'

# Discussion

This study found that a group of patients with SEED-AN consistently scored
similarly to severely depressed primary care patients in subjective appraisal
of quality of life. Consistent with this was a strong correlation between
depressed mood and quality of life. In fact, depressed mood accounted
for variance in scores for quality of life better than either eating disorder
symptoms or BMI scores. The themes of intrapersonal avoidance and self-
punishment/denial in the qualitative data fit with the poor WHOQOL-
100 psychological scores and high BDI scores. The study also found that
some of the living skills of those with SEED-AN were as impaired as that
of a standardized community sample of patients with schizophrenia. The
participants with SEED-AN scored highly for communication skills and
responsibility on the LSP. However, they achieved low scores in self-care
and social contact. The qualitative theme of interpersonal avoidance may
help explain how participants achieve such poor scores in WHOQOL-100
social relations and in LSP social contact despite scoring very highly on LSP
communication skills. The qualitative theme of punishment/denial may
help explain some of the poor score in LSP for self-care. Physical symptoms
did not feature greatly in the qualitative data. This fits with the finding
that BMI scores did not correlate significantly with the physical component
of WHOQOL-100. A participant with Anorexia Nervosa may present as
articulate and well groomed despite severe social isolation and self-neglect.
The LSP scores are more sensitive to the markers of self-neglect seen in

psychosis, such as deterioration in personal hygiene. The qualitative data better identifies the self-denial, guilt and self-punishment that underpin this self-neglect. The LSP mismatch between communication and social contact scores in the participants with Anorexia Nervosa may be better explained by the qualitative data, which describes interpersonal avoidance rather than lack of skills driving the isolation. This indicates a need for an assessment tool, which is validated specifically for participants with eating disorders. Participants' reports documented in the qualitative part of the study details the powerfully positive role that the illness plays in the life of the sufferer, as well as the negative impact of the illness on mental state, family and social life. SEED-AN has been identified as one form of SEED (Robinson, 2006b). This group of conditions, which has yet to be fully characterized, is comparable to other severe psychiatric disorders in their impact on multiple domains of functioning and in their requirement for complex and long-term therapeutic interventions. The present study provides support to this concept and suggests that comparisons can usefully be made between SEED and chronic affective and psychotic disorders.

The numbers in this pilot study were too small for meaningful quantitative statistical analysis. However, if 20% of cases of anorexia develop chronic symptoms then 4 in 100 000 females between 10 and 39 years may go on to develop chronic symptoms. This calls for a differentiated, specialist mental health service, which includes a rehabilitation focused as well as an acute model, such as occurs in general adult psychiatry.

# 8

# A Comparison between SEED and Chronic Schizophrenia

The problems of the patient with treatment resistant chronic schizophrenia are the remit of rehabilitation psychiatry, and the shortcomings of the services provided for this very needy group of people are well described by Holloway (2005). Rehabilitation psychiatry (or rehabilitation and social psychiatry as the Faculty of the Royal College of Psychiatrists is known) largely confines itself to one diagnosis, schizophrenia, with the inclusion of a few individuals with brain damage and autism. The justification for this position is that these patients formed a large proportion of the residents of large psychiatric hospitals, most of which have disappeared over the last 40 years, to be replaced by what Holloway creatively calls the 'virtual hospital', a network of poorly coordinated services in public and private sectors attempting to maximize the level of functioning of their clients, keep them taking their medicines, protect them from their self-damaging behaviours and protect the general population from those among the group who appear to represent a threat. Holloway's paper (2005) persuasively and rightly argues for better coordination of the myriad services that form the virtual hospital.

The plight of the patient with a diagnosis other than schizophrenia who continues to experience symptoms of the disorder is not addressed by the rehabilitation (and recently the recovery) movement, but perhaps these people, with severe eating disorders, obsessional disorders, personality disorders and depression, require an analogous approach, but probably not an identical one. In this chapter, the helpful account of psychiatric rehabilitation provided by Thornton, Seeman and Plummer (2007) is used as a basis for comparing the two sets of conditions. Rather than trying and showing that one or other is 'worse', the aim is to use the extensive experience gained

*Severe and Enduring Eating Disorder*   Paul Robinson
© 2009 John Wiley & Sons, Ltd

in the development of the rehabilitation field in schizophrenia, and begin to apply it to SEED.

In Chapter 7, some preliminary data were presented to show that there appear to be many similarities in quality of life and living skills measures between patients with SEED and those with other chronic psychiatric disorders. There were some differences, however, in communication and responsibility, and a large study comparing SEED with other disorders would clearly be helpful.

The chapter is organized as follows:

1. Interventions from multidisciplinary teams (see Table 8.1).
2. Symptoms of disorder and their management.
3. Areas requiring attention from individual MDT members.
4. *Occupational needs. Avocational needs. Vocational needs.*

## Interventions from Multidisciplinary Teams

### *Medical*

Medication review is relevant to both groups, although the efficacy of medication in schizophrenia in reducing symptoms and preventing relapse is much better established than in eating disorders. Use of antidepressants in eating disorders to suppress bulimic symptoms has some rationale, and they are also commonly used to treat depressive symptoms, almost universal in SEED (see Chapter 6). A Cochrane Review (Claudino *et al.*, 2006) concluded that, while there was insufficient quality data to be sure, there was no significant effect of antidepressants on weight, depression or anxiety in Anorexia Nervosa, in seven studies with a total of 178 participants. The use of antipsychotic drugs, especially olanzapine, is becoming more common, perhaps in the almost certainly vain hope that the weight gaining side effects of the drug will act on anorexic drive for thinness, and perhaps by the curious thought that the body image disturbances are 'a bit psychotic'. This odd conclusion might be related to the confusing use of the word psychotic to mean *deluded and hallucinated* to psychiatrists[1] and *very disturbed* to

---

[1]'Psychosis: Fundamental derangement of the mind (as in schizophrenia) characterized by defective or lost contact with reality especially as evidenced by delusions, hallucinations, and disorganized speech and behaviour.' Merriam-Webster online dictionary, www.merriam-webster.com (accessed 8 June 2008).

**Table 8.1** Interventions in different areas in schizophrenia compared to SEED

| Intervention | SZA | SEED | Staff involved | Comments: SZA vs SEED |
|---|---|---|---|---|
| Medical | Medication | Nutrition | Medical, nursing, dietetic (any) | No medication currently improves outcome in SEED-AN |
| Follow-up | Symptom and medication review | Physical monitoring | Medical, nursing, dietetic (any) | Risk management in both |
| Crisis intervention | Hospitalization, crisis care | Outreach and day care, inpatient care | Any + medical | Similar |
| Psychological intervention | Supportive psychotherapy | Supportive psychotherapy | Group or individual therapist | No specific therapy effective in either |
| Management of substance misuse | Supportive therapy, substance misuse service | Supportive therapy, substance misuse service (SMS) | Any + SMS | Probably less in SEED |
| Attention to basic needs: shelter, food, clothing, spending money | Care coordination, social work | Care coordination, social work | Any | Apart from food, less of a problem in SEED |

123

psychoanalysts[2]. The patients are certainly alarmed when they study the nutritional side effects on the drug information leaflet.

## Follow-up

While medication review should probably be done by a medically qualified person, the follow-up can be performed by any health care professional, preferably someone who knows the patient well. Follow-up in psychiatric and other medical services is often performed by someone who is due to spend 6 months in the job, and may only see the patient once or twice which makes the process difficult and not particularly satisfactory for both clinician and patient. This is not a very high priority for research grants, but it may be that seeing the same trusted person every few weeks, over several years, can lead to a healthy attachment, perhaps making up for previous inadequate or abusive attachments. If so, then follow-up may have an importance similar to psychotherapy, in which such healthy attachments are fostered and probably account for improvements in therapy, whatever model is used. Follow-up should therefore be with the same person, at predictable intervals and sessions should be for an agreed period of time, which might vary between 20 and 60 minutes. The content is likely to be a clinical review of the patient's state and discussion of possible changes as well as family issues and stressful events. The assessment of risk, whether to self or others, form an important part of such follow-ups, for people with any psychiatric disorder, although physical assessment needs to be particularly considered in SEED.

## Crisis intervention

A crisis may present as inability to cope, increasing distress, suicidal or homicidal intentions, increasing behavioural disorder or physical symptoms and signs which indicate serious risk to health. Clearly, the latter is more common in SEED than in schizophrenia, in which the former are more

---

[2]For example, 'Psychotic defenses are psychic processes involving unconscious, or more-or-less conscious, attempts to deal with reality. They take the form of disavowal or withdrawal as the subject tries to avoid or circumscribe conflicts encountered in his relationship with the external world.' International Dictionary of Psychoanalysis, www.enotes.com/psychoanalysis-encyclopedia (accessed 8 June 2008).

common. Our response depends on the level of risk and its nature, and the options are increased community support, involvement of a crisis response team, admission to a crisis house or admission to a medical or psychiatric inpatient ward. A patient with SEED may be destabilized by a significant life event, or a predictable event such as Christmas, as can someone with schizophrenia.

## Psychological intervention

When they get to the stage of chronic illness, some patients have had therapy till it is coming out of their ears. This is more true of patients with eating disorders than psychosis. Psychotherapy in stable SEED is usually best targeted at specific difficulties, such as the emergence of phobias in a patient with SEED who did not have them before, or at eating disorder symptoms such as bulimia or low weight which, by some accident, have not previously been treated. When SEED becomes unstable, for example if weight falls, then all treatments are justified to try and help the patient increase weight again. In schizophrenia, the same principles apply, and although rehabilitation may well include psychological treatments such as CBT and occasionally reinforcement approaches, a vital ingredient of treatment, not available in eating disorders, is to foster compliance with medication known to reduce the risk of relapse.

## Management of substance misuse

Because of the effects of illicit drugs on behaviour, symptoms, compliance, drug interactions and illness relapse, this area is of particular importance in schizophrenia and the term 'dual diagnosis' is often taken to mean 'psychosis with substance misuse'. Some of the problems apply to SEED, but the area is of less prominence. Amphetamines and cocaine are sometimes taken to reduce appetite and improve social life and can make rehabilitation more difficult because of their effects on motivation. Cannabis has a tendency to cause overeating ('the munchies'), but is still commonly used, especially by patients with bulimia. Alcohol, especially when taken in large alcoholic binges, is often followed by bulimic episodes and the cyclical sequence drink–binge–starve is a familiar one. Patients with drug or alcohol misuse, causing serious disruption in symptoms or in rehabilitation, can be asked to contact substance misuse services or self-help organizations for assistance.

*Attention to basic needs*

Few patients with eating disorders are homeless. Some are in temporary accommodation, sometimes as students, but eating disorders do not usually cause such a marked downward social drift as does chronic schizophrenia. The problems of finance and housing that do occur are discussed below, under Section 3.

## Symptoms of Disorder and Their Management (Table 8.2)

*Positive symptoms*

Just as patients with schizophrenia have hallucinatory voices and delusional convictions that have a significant control over their behaviour, patients with SEED have thoughts and beliefs that almost completely control their behaviour. Unfortunately, there are no mind-altering drugs which can reduce a feeling of fatness. It is not such an odd idea, considering that we do have drugs that can stop you from thinking that the government is out to control you (a great achievement in the days of biometric identity cards and one security camera for every 50 Londoners). Still, the physician treating schizophrenia does have a great advantage. There is treatment which works to some extent, and so monitoring compliance is worthwhile. In SEED, especially the underweight variety, we await the treatment that will reduce patients' longing to be thinner. It will probably be multidimensional and mainly psychosocial, but gene therapy to switch on (or off) excessive satiety signalling will not be turned away.

*Negative symptoms*

The negative symptoms of SEED are, in a way, the most debilitating. They can be understood partly as the results of being ill for a long time (secondary handicaps) or as additional illness including depression and obsessive compulsive disorder that constrict life and reduce its quality. They include social withdrawal and social isolation. Schizophrenic negative symptoms also include social withdrawal and isolation, and arise from poor motivation, a reduction in the range and expression of affect ('flattening') and thought disorder, although the latter is sometimes thought of as a positive symptom. The effects are rather similar, the patient having few social contacts,

**Table 8.2** Different types of symptoms in schizophrenia compared to SEED

| Symptom group | SZA | SEED | Comments |
|---|---|---|---|
| Positive symptoms | Delusions, hallucinations, odd behaviour | Body image disturbance, bulimic symptoms, odd behaviour around food | Different range of symptoms |
| Negative symptoms | Loss of interest, energy, warmth, humour | Social withdrawal, obsessional symptoms, depression | |
| Personal care needs: hygiene, personal safety, medical care, mobility | Hygiene problems, self-neglect, physical illnesses, obesity | Self-neglect, self-harm, malnutrition, osteoporosis, fractures | In SEED, malnutrition is the patient's aim |
| Nutrition | Drug-induced obesity, lack of exercise | Inadequate food, purging behaviours, excess exercise | Obesity major problem in SZA, emaciation in AN |

sometimes restricted to health care professionals, and sometimes a few patients, leading to impoverished lives. Some drugs may influence these symptoms in schizophrenia, but as in SEED, the treatment usually provided is to encourage the patient to make social contacts, join appropriate classes or attend a rehabilitation or day centre.

*Personal care needs*

In schizophrenia, the patient may require help to increase motivation to keep him- or herself clean and sweet smelling. Patients with eating disorders are often meticulous about their habits. However, their behaviour may cause people around to avoid them if not comment. Smells of vomit in the toilet are common, and less common, but more alarming are bags of vomit left in the bedroom, or, sometimes, in strategic places in the home for relatives to discover. Misuse of laxatives can lead to faecal incontinence, and long-term laxative abuse in someone low in weight can cause rectal prolapse and long-term incontinence of urine and faeces due to weakness of the pelvic floor muscles. This occurs rarely, however (although it might appear more common if we asked about it routinely), and the most important self-care problems in patients with SEED are consequences of low weight, namely weakness, physical illness and osteoporosis. Different physical problems abound in patients with schizophrenia, including obesity, lung disease and diabetes.

## Areas Requiring Attention from Individual MDT Members (Tables 8.3, 8.4, 8.5)

These areas may be addressed by individual team members, who may be social workers, occupational therapists, nurses or, at times, therapists.

*Social benefits*

Patients with schizophrenia are sometimes too disorganized to claim state benefits and for this reason may end up as vagrants. Those with eating disorders usually have the capacity to claim, but for various reasons do not. These reasons include guilt at not being able to earn, not feeling worthy

**Table 8.3** Psychosocial needs in schizophrenia and SEED—1

| | Schizophrenia | SEED | Comments |
|---|---|---|---|
| Social benefits | Symptoms may impair ability to apply | Patient may be reluctant to claim | In SZA, problem is disorganization; in AN, depression and low self-esteem |
| Budgeting | May be hard to organize, poverty | Clinical frugality in AN, overspending in borderline PD | Poverty more significant in SZA |
| Housing | Availability, stigma, poverty | Little available for patient with severe malnutrition | Stigma in SZA, inability to eat enough in AN |
| Nutrition | Drug-induced obesity, lack of exercise | Inadequate food, purging behaviours, excess exercise | Obesity main problem in SZA, emaciation in AN |
| Interpersonal relationships | Social difficulties, isolation, suspicion of others | Inability to eat out, lack of libido, fears of relationships | Social isolation in both for very different reasons |
| Emotional/spiritual support | Isolation from friends and family, religious affiliation | Support based on eating disorder. Alienation from friends/family due to ED behaviours. Sometimes religious affiliation is enhanced | Symptomatic behaviours impair social relations in both |
| Daily recreational activities | Loss of social activities, hobbies, family | Eating disorder may exclude other activities | Negative symptoms in SZA, primacy of ED in SEED |
| Vocational activities | Problems concentrating, working with others | Years out of work, poor physical health | More of a problem in SZA; some very low SEED patients surprisingly in work. |

**Table 8.4** Psychosocial needs in schizophrenia and SEED—2

| | Schizophrenia | SEED | Comments |
|---|---|---|---|
| Basic living skills: communication, shopping, cooking, taking a bus, etc. | Can be affected | Cooking problematic, obsessional aspects | Problem in SZA general; in SEED specific to food and exercise |
| Transport | Cost; may require travel pass | Travel pass justified due to poor physical health and exercise addiction | Travel pass often difficult to get in SEED |
| Use of leisure: local activities, social events, groups for ex-psychiatric patients, day programmes, visits from professionals, exercise, athletic activities | May be required due to social exclusion, depression, suspiciousness; athletics useful to combat weight gain | May be required due to social isolation, effect of behavioural symptoms; athletic activities may pose problems due to exercise addiction | Stigma important in both; symptoms may appear odd or unacceptable to public |
| Domestic activities: shopping, cooking, cleaning | Problems due to poor motivation etc. and lack of skills | Required due to ambivalence about food, obsessive rituals | Patients with SEED are sometimes obsessive about cleaning, rituals around food |
| Phone services | To help social and professional contact | To help social and professional contact | Less problematic in SEED |

**Table 8.5** Psychosocial needs in schizophrenia and SEED—3

| | Schizophrenia | SEED | Comments |
|---|---|---|---|
| Trips away | To combat social isolation and boredom; may need to be organized | Patients more capable of organizing trips themselves | But eating away is often problematic, so trips are avoided |
| Help in caring for children | Children can act as young carers and also be affected by parent's behaviour; support and monitoring of children necessary | Children may have growth and behavioural problems; may act as young carers; support and monitoring essential | Important in both |
| Physical fitness | Problems due to e.g. lack of exercise and smoking | Problems due to poor nutrition, smoking, osteoporosis | Both have impaired life expectancy |
| Spiritual counselling | Helpful for some individuals | Helpful for some individuals | Ascetic self-denial in SEED sometimes applauded |
| Creative outlets | Art, music, writing useful; in talented individual interesting results | Yes, but danger of 'clinical perfectionism' | Patients with SEED may avoid art, music, etc. for fear of not meeting standards |

to claim, shame at claiming and a feeling that they are not really ill and could earn if necessary. Some may not claim for reasons of asceticism, which coincide with a wish to minimize eating and these days, with a green tendency, consuming as few resources as possible, all of which are seen in patients with eating disorders. In addition, some fail to claim for a free travel pass, wishing to maximize energy expended by walking. Moreover, some families, failing to realize the disabilities with which the patient is struggling, insist on her applying for a job, rather than for state benefits. As a result, some patients with SEED are very short of money, and have a monkish existence which perpetuates and worsens their nutritional state. A few with better-off families retain the status of a dependent child by having their bills paid by parents.

## Budgeting

While patients with schizophrenia may have difficulty budgeting because of a small income compounded by the effects of symptoms, as well as the costs of habits such as smoking, those with eating disorders are often extremely organized in this domain. Their difficulties arise from either an unwillingness to spend money, as a result of *clinical frugality* (see Chapter 4), or excessive expenditure which may be due to the cost of funding bulimic episodes, or more rarely overspending in a patient with elevated mood. Smoking, as an appetite suppressant, is also common in the eating disordered population. Some frugal patients may have been on benefits and hardly spent anything, accumulating a substantial amount in the bank, which can then lead to cuts in those benefits when the nest egg is discovered! They may then have difficulty spending the money in their bank accounts because it represents the security they lack in their inner and outer lives.

## Housing

Patients with chronic schizophrenia may have difficulty finding a house because their condition may have alienated family and friends, they may have a low income, and suffer from stigma when they try and find accommodation. Their illness may demand that they have access to staff on site, and so need supported accommodation, which is scarce, although investment in community care has led to a marked increase in such facilities. The majority of patients with SEED stay either with their parents, for whom they may eventually become carers, or in their own accommodation, often a single occupancy flat, supplied by the local council, or sometimes privately rented or owned. Patients with SEED who require supported accommodation are in two groups: those with recurrent weight loss due to Anorexia Nervosa and those with serious psychiatric and physical co-morbidity, as illustrated in the following two vignettes.

In this first case, a hostel for people with eating disorders delayed readmission substantially:

*Patient W suffered from Anorexia Nervosa from the age of 18 when she lost weight rapidly after leaving home to attend college. Over the next 13 years she spent much time in hospital, losing weight rapidly after discharge and requiring urgent readmission. After two admissions, she maintained weight for longer than average. The first was early in her illness when she was living at home, and attending an intensive day service. The second was later in the illness when she was admitted to a hostel exclusively for people with eating disorders where she stayed for 2 years before losing weight again and requiring readmission.*

In this case, a patient with serious co-morbidity was suitable for but has not yet entered supported accommodation:

### Patient I

*This 42-year-old woman suffered from Anorexia Nervosa and obsessive compulsive disorder since the age of 16 and epilepsy since 12. She abused laxatives for many years and as a result had recurrent rectal prolapse and multiple medical problems for which she consulted many physicians and surgeons. Her obsessionality led her to keep every piece of paper she received and as a result her one-roomed flat was littered to a depth of 50 cm with piles of paper, through which paths to her bed and toilet had been cleared. She resisted all attempts to clear the flat and was several times admitted to hospital with severe emaciation due to self-neglect. In her latest admission she has agreed to rehousing and for some time was unable to cooperate with steps to arrange it, apparently preferring to live in hospital. She has subsequently left hospital for supported accommodation.*

Sadly there are, in the United Kingdom, very few supported hostels catering for people with eating disorders, and when services are willing to try and take on the challenges of caring for someone who seeks to avoid adequate nutrition as far as possible, they may lack information and skills to help the patient avoid further weight loss and rehospitalization.

Patients with SEED in their own accommodation can benefit substantially from community mental health team and primary care support, including medical review and regular, sometimes weekly, support worker visits, which can help the patient cope in the community. Eating disorder services can provide a monitoring role with an appointment every few weeks. Many generic teams are willing to adopt this role, which is to provide services for all patients with severe and enduring mental illness in their area. Some, however, do what they can to avoid this work, and may even try and withdraw from the care of the patient altogether. This is often inappropriate, although given the pressures on generic teams it may be understandable. The problem is that the eating disorder teams, which can provide intensive therapy and support in the acute phase, perhaps the first 2 years after referral, are inadequately staffed to build up a large caseload of chronically ill patients and need to work with the local teams to make sure the patients' needs are met. Mostly this occurs amicably, but not always.

## Nutrition

In schizophrenia, nutrition can sometimes be impaired as a result of general self-neglect and sometimes due to delusions concerning food or poisoning. The most common problem is overnutrition, related to poor diet, lack of exercise and side effects of medication. This, and the effects of smoking, contribute to the large burden of health problems borne by these patients. The response of health services is often inadequate. Dietary advice and exercise programmes are sometimes provided, but are not high priorities for funding. Occasionally, such patients are referred for consideration for bariatric surgery. To benefit from such interventions, the patient needs to be in a stable state and able to comply with quite demanding post-operative dietary advice and outpatient care. In SEED, the majority suffer from undernutrition, as a result of dietary restriction, excess exercise and purging behaviours. As these problems are the defining ones for the conditions, interventions are the treatment for the eating disorder, namely medical and dietary consultation, psychological therapies and nutritional support when required. In both psychosis and SEED, long-term dietary inadequacy can be associated with micronutrient deficiency, and while an abnormal full blood count can point to some of the associated conditions such as iron, B12 and folate deficiency, a more certain, if blunderbuss, approach is to prescribe a daily dose of a multi-vitamin such as Forceval or an equivalent preparation. For patients at risk for osteoporosis, including those with chronic low weight and possibly those on long-term neuroleptics, some advocate daily calcium and vitamin D, although evidence on the efficacy of calcium in preventing bone loss in Anorexia Nervosa is lacking.

## *Interpersonal relationships, emotional support*

Both schizophrenia and SEED affect the capacity to establish and maintain relationships including those in the family, in friendship circles and in sexual relationships. The reasons are different and in the first group include depression and poor motivation, the quality of social skills and the degree of fear and stigma in society. In the case of SEED, restrictive eating habits, depression and reduced drive, a wish for solitude (often accompanied by a powerful need for human contact) and fear of sexuality all conspire to restrict social life. In both cases, contact with health care professionals and other patients may form the bulk of the patients' social activities. It is important not to encourage the patient to place him- or herself in a frightening and unduly challenging situation, and improvements in social engagement are best made gradually with the patient leading. The team member helping the patient can be from any profession, and the patient will make his or her own choice as to which team member is most suitable for a particular discussion:

### Patient X

*A 33-year-old woman with a 17-year history of anorexia and bulimia nervosa consulted her psychiatrist because she had, for the first time, agreed to go out on a date with a male friend, and had never discussed sex with an adult. She asked the (male) doctor numerous questions about what to expect, and a discussion very like one between a parent and an adolescent child ensued.*

Activities in which social contact may be fostered can range from day centres and self-help groups to evening classes, sheltered workshops and, for the IT literate, social internet sites such as Facebook. The team member chosen to take on this role can encourage, advise and be ready to administer first aid, should an attempt founder.

## Daily recreational activities

In someone with a restricted social network, opportunities for recreation are limited to solitary activities, and this applies to anyone with a long-term psychiatric disorder. The patient with SEED may be more likely to take an activity, such as cycling to excess, as a result of perfectionism and a wish to waste calories. Although depression, negative symptoms of schizophrenia and physical weakness may contribute to a tendency to avoid activity, in the patient with Anorexia Nervosa, muscle wasting is often overwhelmed by a huge capacity for exercise which seems to reside in the patient's compulsion to get rid of the nutritional value of any food ingested. Such people may continue to remain hyperactive until they are in a state of collapse due to malnutrition.

## Daily vocational activities

Capacity to work is probably more impaired in schizophrenia than in SEED, except for the most severely ill underweight patients who spend little time outside hospital. Both, however, can benefit from work in a sheltered environment for people who have been through the mental health system, where expectations are geared to the problems faced by people with chronic psychiatric disorder, whether it is difficulty concentrating, communicating, dealing with food or having enough motivation to complete a task. However, there has to be a balance struck so that expectations are high enough to prepare the patient for employment in the wider world at the end of the period at the workshop.

One is surprised to find some patients with SEED at work:

### Patient Y

*A 45-year-old woman with a 23-year history of Anorexia Nervosa was working as a receptionist at a doctors' practice. She had been at a BMI of 9.5 for some years and had the impression that some of the doctors' patients, on seeing how ill she looked when they arrived at the reception desk, reconsidered their need for an appointment and went away.*

Sometimes, a combination of an eating disorder and psychosis leads to admission to a psychosis rehabilitation service:

### Patient Z

*This 35-year-old woman developed anorexia and bulimia nervosa at 16, requiring several admissions for extreme emaciation, with BMI falling to 10.5. On the third admission, after discharge at a BMI of 16, she developed paranoid delusions and hallucinations that were 'anorexic' in content, e.g. that the Coca Cola company were lacing the can of Diet Coke she was due to drink with sugar to make her put on weight. Over a number of years her eating disorder symptoms receded, but she developed negative symptoms of schizophrenia, with lack of motivation and thought disorder as well as a chronically deluded and hallucinated state. There was a reasonable response to antipsychotic medication, but she failed to take it as prescribed. She was admitted to a rehabilitation ward where she remains, 3 years after her last eating disorders admission.*

*Comment on Patient Z.* This patient developed schizophrenia after suffering from very severe Anorexia Nervosa. The initial psychotic symptoms were anorexic in content. They followed a period of severe malnutrition, and it is theoretically possible that inadequate cerebral energy supply may have led to brain damage contributing to a chronic psychotic illness. The association of Anorexia Nervosa accompanied by psychotic symptoms with clear eating disorder content may be termed *anorexia psychosa*.

## Occupational Needs[3] (Table 8.6)

### Avocational needs

*Basic living skills*    Communication may be less problematic in patients with SEED than in schizophrenia, because of the nature of the conditions. Shopping may be impaired by difficulties in motivation and decision making in schizophrenia and by frugality, obsessionality, depression and, in clothes and food shopping, eating disorder considerations in SEED. Housework may be impaired in both, but the patient with SEED is often found to be performing housework excessively. Using public transport can provide challenges to someone with cognitive impairment which occurs in schizophrenia

---

[3] Some have been considered above, but are left in the lists for completeness.

**Table 8.6** Vocational rehabilitation in schizophrenia and SEED

| Vocational rehab | Schizophrenia | SEED | Comments |
| --- | --- | --- | --- |
| Employment | Loss of skills, effects of symptoms, medication, time out | Effects of physical and psychological symptoms, time out | More problematic in SZA |
| Special programmes for mentally ill workers | Useful as stepping stone to work | Often useful; patient may deny problems and attempt too much | Difficult to persuade patients with SEED to try due to self-imposed stigma |
| Volunteer work | Useful initial step | Useful, but rejected often as too basic | Relevant in both |
| Retraining: vocational, non-vocational, correspondence | Depending on degree of psychosocial impairment | Patients may deny impairment and aim too high | Patients with SEED more likely to have higher education; both groups may be distracted by symptoms |

(Elvevåg and Goldberg, 2000). Someone with SEED and muscle weakness may have trouble with long staircases at underground stations, and may also find the jerky movements of a bus difficult to cope with, risking a fracture in case of a fall:

> *Transport.* This has been mentioned above, as has the reluctance, sometimes, for patients with SEED to claim a free travel pass.
>
> *Use of leisure.* Mentioned in the previous section.
>
> *Domestic activities.* Housework and cooking have been considered.
>
> *Phone and Internet services.* Negotiating the jungle of provider services and deals may require assistance, perhaps more in psychosis than SEED.
>
> *Spiritual counselling.* The health care worker who does not hold religious beliefs should not ignore the needs in this area of a patient with a mental disorder. Many patients find work in a religious establishment to be rewarding and somewhere that they find rare acceptance of their difficulties. This probably applies equally to both groups of patients under consideration.
>
> *Creative outlets.* This has also been discussed. It is important to be aware that however pervasive a mental disorder seems, there are often areas such as skills learnt that can still find expression, as creative therapists are aware. Some patients with schizophrenia can overcome their general lack of motivation if one area of skill, such as art or singing, can be tapped. Similarly, if a patient with SEED can overcome inhibitions due to perfectionism and anticipated failure and embark on a project in which skills such as drawing can be exploited, an important source of self-esteem, and perhaps occupation, can be discovered.
>
> *Trips away.* These are problematic for both groups of patients. For those with schizophrenia, fear of embarking on unfamiliar territory with unknown people, together with negative and positive symptoms, make outings away from home potentially threatening. For those with eating disorders, the constant fear is of unfamiliar food with unknown nutritional content as well as a general distaste for change and loss of complete control of one's lifestyle, militating against trips away, especially holidays. Conversely, some patients with bulimia nervosa take a holiday from their symptoms while they are away.
>
> *Help in caring for children.* In parental mental disorders, children are recognized as at risk because of neglect and abuse, and because of the problems of being a young carer. These concerns apply to a proportion of people with any serious mental disorder. In eating disorders,

however, there is a risk of the nutrition of a child being specifically impaired because of the abnormal attitudes to food and body weight in the mother. Thus, general help is required for all people with serious mental disorder who have young children, and in the case of women with eating disorders, special help is needed to monitor the development of the baby, and to handle vulnerable times, especially mealtimes, which can be very fraught for both the mother with the eating disorder and the baby.

*Physical fitness.* In schizophrenia, as already discussed, there is an excess of life-style induced illness, including those related to smoking, obesity and poor physical fitness. Sometimes, help is provided to these patients to stop smoking, eat more healthily and take more exercise, but too little is done. In SEED, physical fitness is more likely related to malnutrition, as discussed above.

## Vocational needs

*Employment.* Discussed above.

*Special programmes for mentally ill workers.* Discussed above.

*Volunteer work.* Volunteering, whether it is helping in a charity shop, distributing food to the destitute, helping a reading-impaired child or any of the many available roles, can be an extremely helpful step in rehabilitation with a mental disorder. Some patients with high previous professional achievement may be reluctant to embark on such tasks that they define as 'menial'. However, they can often be persuaded and greatly benefit from the social contact, the achievement and the relative lack of pressure in such an occupation. Patients with eating disorders and clinical perfectionism may reject anything but their former occupation as not good enough, and they also need to be persuaded by the stepping stone model. It is useful to make contact with people responsible for managing such projects, so that expectations can be predicted and managed.

*Retraining.* Vocational, non-vocational, correspondence.

As already discussed, sheltered training as well as general training courses in relevant skills, including IT, can be very helpful, even if a patient already has a vocational training, because they can re-introduce someone who may have been out of the workplace for several years, back into the world of work which has almost certainly changed significantly. Patients with eating disorders tend to be attracted to courses and work which involve food, such as cooking or dietetics, or psychology, such as counselling. This seems to be a reflection of their preoccupations, which in turn are due to the state of starvation or bulimic symptoms. It is not necessarily something that should be dissuaded as 'part of the illness'. There is no evidence that people with eating disorders make worse cooks or counsellors than those without, although the eating disorder may distort their work, perhaps overfeeding their restaurant clients, or conveying a distorted body image to an eating disordered counselling client.

# 9

# 99 Research Ideas

In this chapter, I offer suggestions for research projects arranged according to the chapter in which the issue comes up in the hope that some of them will be taken up. I have included some relatively simple projects suitable for student dissertations (marked S). If several of these ideas are taken up and preliminary data obtained, a symposium on SEED could take place within 2–3 years, perhaps addressing some of the issues raised. Some of the ideas are vaguely expressed, others more specific. Some have been researched to a certain point and require a larger, more definitive study.

## Chapter 1: Introduction

Severe and enduring eating disorders (SEED) is a concept that has been developing for some years, as it has been clearly recognized that eating disorders can be just as debilitating and disabling as other serious mental disorders. Moreover, the dimension of physical problems gives patients with SEED an additional range of problems which can interact with the psychological. Because SEED is an idea which has emerged from clinical practice, it requires research backing before it can be accepted as valid. Some of the projects suggested are, indeed, aimed at looking at the concept, and examining the possibility that there may be a discontinuity between patients whose illness has gone on for 5 years and those who have been ill for 15 years. Whether a clear boundary at the suggested 10 years or otherwise can be found is unknown:

*Severe and Enduring Eating Disorder*    Paul Robinson
© 2009 John Wiley & Sons, Ltd

1. SEED as a concept: rates of recovery and of complications including death in patients with eating disorders of different duration and symptoms.
2. Stigma of eating disorder diagnosis in psychiatric and medical settings.
3. Validation of the blame spectrum.
4. Handicap and adaptation in eating disorders.
5. Primary and secondary handicaps.
6. Long-term monitoring of SEED in primary care: what to measure, when.
7. Complexity theory as applied to eating disorders.
8. Compare SEED with other chronic psychiatric and physical disorders.
9. Number of patients with SEED treated primarily in general psychiatric services (S).

## Chapter 2: Psychiatric Aspects

There is substantial controversy about the classification and phenomenology of eating disorders. EDNOS has been a very difficult concept to use, because it is heterogeneous and extremely common. The body image disturbance sometimes appears so strong as to be difficult to distinguish from a delusion (or a hallucination), but most psychiatrists sense that they are different. Hunger, satiety and their interaction with changes in gastric function are not well understood. Moreover, the boundaries of eating disorders are unclear, where they overlap with substance misuse, borderline personality disorder and obesity:

1. Comparison of eating attitudes and behaviour in SEED and in other forms of malnutrition.
2. Validation of the short- and long-term starvation concepts in bulimia nervosa.
3. Study of *eking behaviour* in eating disorders.
4. Causes and consequences of delayed gastric emptying in eating disorders.
5. Study of the survival advantage of delayed gastric emptying during food shortage.
6. Phenomenology of body image disturbance in SEED.

7. Comparison of patients' and health care workers' beliefs about the effects of laxatives on food absorption and weight (S).
8. Aetiology of obsessive compulsive symptoms in SEED.
9. A descriptive study of self-harming behaviours on eating disorder inpatient units (S).
10. Developing a coherent approach to patients with long-term eating disorders complicated by borderline personality disorder.
11. Developing a coherent assessment for patients with combinations of different psychiatric disorders including eating disorders, substance misuse and personality disorder.
12. Withdrawal of Fluoxetine in patients with chronic bulimia nervosa: rates of recurrence of bulimia symptoms.
13. Overlap between chronic eating disorders and body dysmorphic disorder.

## Chapter 3: Medical Aspects

Thousands of papers have been written on the physical consequences of eating disorders; almost all concluding that the changes seen in hormones, solutes, stomach, bowel and brain were secondary to malnutrition and the other symptoms of eating disorders. Nevertheless, many important questions remain. How do we assess risk in someone with severe Anorexia Nervosa? How should a GP respond to a patient who is clearly underweight, requesting a referral to an allergy specialist? Other areas which could be explored include disorders of almost every bodily system, with only a fraction of the possible studies mentioned here:

1. Risk seeking in eating disorders. Qualitative study (S).
2. Stability of physical measures and risk to life in eating disorders.
3. Evidence for allergies, IBS and food intolerance in patients with eating disorders diagnosed with these complaints.
4. Allergy specialists, nutritionists and dietary restriction: a potential for conflict between treatment of allergies and eating disorders.
5. Prevalence of somatoform disorder in chronic eating disorders and impact of each on the other.
6. Effect of chronic laxative abuse on absorption of a variety of foods.
7. Impact of laxative abuse on body water (S).

8. Laxative abuse and intestinal dysmotility: changes in reversibility with time.
9. Causes of raised transaminase levels in eating disorders.
10. Intestinal permeability in low weight patients with raised transaminase levels.
11. Reliability and validity of the SUSS test in patients underweight due to eating and other disorders (S).
12. Creatine Kinase isoenzymes in Anorexia Nervosa, cardiac status and relation to exercise.
13. ECG changes in eating disorders due to low weight and electrolyte disturbance.
14. Models of co-management of very ill patients by nutrition physicians and eating disorder specialists.
15. Body water, electrolytes and capillary permeability in patients with eating disorders and oedema.
16. Endocrine function in patients with eating disorders and oedema including electrolyte and endocrine changes.
17. Management of oedema in AN/BN.
18. Treatment with calcium and vitamin D and oestrogen in osteoporosis due to Anorexia Nervosa.
19. Biphosphonates in men with osteoporosis due to Anorexia Nervosa.
20. Exercise in Anorexia Nervosa: effects on recovery, depression and bone density.
21. Gastro-oesophageal reflux in bulimia: time course of recovery of sphincter function after cessation of vomiting.
22. Proton pump inhibitor treatment of gastro-oesophageal reflux in bulimia nervosa.
23. Capillary permeability in AN or BN (S).
24. Fertility in low weight patients with SEED. Does menstrual weight fall with time?
25. Basal calorie requirements in patients with eating disorders with varied chronicity and symptom spectrum.
26. Rates of undisclosed urinary and faecal incontinence in eating disorders (S).
27. Pelvic floor weakness in Anorexia Nervosa and laxative abuse.
28. A study of patients with SEED in primary care: rates of and reasons for consultations.

# Chapter 4: Social and Occupation Aspects

Research in this area extends from psychological studies of attachment and mentalization and behavioural patterns in SEED to the varied accommodation and occupational needs of patients with SEED, and how they might be met by generic and specialist teams:

1. Attachment patterns during childhood in patients who later develop eating disorders.
2. Reflective function in patients with SEED, those with recent onset eating disorders and their relatives.
3. Assessment of accommodation needs of patients with SEED.
4. A survey of involvement of generic psychiatric services in management of patients with SEED.
5. Rehabilitation in SEED: models of care, relative efficacy of specialist and generic provision.
6. Shoplifting of food and non-food items in eating disorders (S).
7. Hoarding in SEED (S).
8. Clinical frugality in eating disorders.
9. Use of skin care products in eating disorders (S).
10. Chronic eating disorders in ex-fashion models, ballet dancers and people from other high-risk occupations.
11. Barriers to employment in eating disorders.
12. The restaurant experience in eating disorders (S).
13. Orthocompulsions in psychiatric and non-psychiatric populations.
14. SEED in offspring of immigrant families. Impact of tension between host and family culture.

# Chapter 5: Family Aspects

Here, the patient's relationship to the family, leaving home, as well as impact of the patient's relationships and children are the subject of a variety of projects:

1. Patients as carers of elderly parents (S).
2. Expressed emotion in families of patients with eating disorders.

3. Quality of attachment in families of patients with eating disorders.
4. Burden and psychiatric disorder in relatives of patients with SEED.
5. Short-term outcome when patients with long-term eating disorders leave home for higher education.
6. Difficulties separating for people with SEED and their parents and carers.
7. Impact of SEED on siblings.
8. Eating and other psychiatric disorders in siblings.
9. Eating behaviour, eating disorders, psychiatric disorder, growth and development in the offspring of parents with eating disorders.
10. Outcome of pregnancies in patients with eating disorders.
11. Eating behaviour and personality characteristics in sexual partners of women with eating disorders.
12. Account of concordant and discordant twins' experience of their eating disorder.
13. Ethical issues in relation to confidentiality for adult patients with eating disorders living with their families.
14. Families with multiple children with eating disorders: a search for genetic and environmental factors.

## Chapter 6: The Care Programme Approach

The Care Programme Approach has long been used in all manner of psychiatric disorders, including SEED. Issues for study include variations in practice, and how transfer between services is managed. CPA was first introduced as a result of a fatal incident occurring when a patient known to one area team moved to another area where he was not known. In the management of SEED, the issues more frequently concern risk to patients from malnutrition and self-harm, when they move between services. These projects cover not only CPA implementation, but some areas that are covered by the process, such as barriers to implementing care plans generated under CPA:

1. A survey of the implementation of the Care Programme Approach in SEED.
2. Problems arising for patients with eating disorders and their families around transfer between inpatient, child and adolescent, adult general, adult specialist, private and public services.

3. Views of patients, relatives and carers of the experience of the CPA process and meeting.
4. Patients', relatives' and carers' desired information in relation to diagnosis.
5. Psychological management of the patient who has had a lot of previous therapy.
6. Impact of time-consuming symptoms on capacity for occupational rehabilitation in SEED.
7. A register of reviewed and quality-assessed Internet resources for people with SEED.
8. Physical symptoms of eating disorders impacting on safety as a car driver.
9. Risk assessment in eating disorders: clinical procedures and appropriate documentation.
10. Criteria for emergency intervention (including the Mental Health Act) in SEED.
11. Models of shared care between primary and secondary care in high-risk patients with SEED.

## Chapter 7: Outcome Measures

Because this chapter was a reproduced study itself, the question of further research is addressed in the text. These two studies, however, suggest themselves:

1. A large study of psychiatric, physical and social outcome in SEED compared with other psychiatric and physical disorders.
2. An assessment of outcome of inpatient care comparing units readily accessible to and far from the patient's home.

## Chapter 8: Comparison with Schizophrenia

The idea of comparing Anorexia Nervosa with schizophrenia might seem inappropriate to some. The small pilot study reproduced in Chapter 7 suggested that quality of life and other measures, were not very different from groups of patients with chronic psychiatric disorders, such as depression. In Chapter 8, schizophrenia, which has been well studied by researchers interested in psychiatric rehabilitation is compared with SEED, a set of conditions with chronic severe physical and psychological symptoms as well as social disturbances. These projects address some of the areas found relevant in the study of schizophrenia:

1. A comparison of psychiatric follow-up from doctors who move posts every 6 months with follow-up from doctors who stay put.
2. A randomized controlled trial of olanzapine in Anorexia Nervosa.
3. Suicidality and the wish to die in patients with SEED.
4. State benefits in SEED, rates of refusal by benefits agencies and failure to apply by patients.
5. Smoking in eating disorders and schizophrenia. Relative impact on physical health.
6. Hostels for people with eating disorders: descriptive and outcome studies.
7. Occupations in which people with SEED can function well. Assessment of modifications to working conditions required to accommodate people with SEED.
8. Religious observance in SEED. Link with asceticism.

# Glossary

*NL: This indicates a neologism (new word) coined by the author*

**Adaptation:** An individual's response to an illness or disability.

**Aldosterone:** A hormone produced in the adrenal gland on top of each kidney which regulates the sodium and potassium content of the body.

**Amenorrhoea:** Cessation of menstrual periods.

**Angiotensin:** A hormone produced in the liver which raises blood pressure by constricting blood vessels and stimulating aldosterone (qv).

**Antidiuretic hormone:** Hormone produced by the pituitary gland in the brain which stimulates the kidney to retain water.

**B-EAT:** A major organization for people with eating disorders and their carers.

**Binge:** Consumption of an objectively large amount of food, generally rapidly, in private, in a time-limited episode accompanied by subjective distress.

**Biphosphonates:** A class of drugs which can improve bone density in osteoporosis (e.g. alendronate).

**Blame spectrum (NL):** The way in which different medical conditions are seen to be more of less the responsibility of the sufferer (e.g. compare alcoholism with leukaemia).

**BMI:** Body Mass Index. The number used to compare adults of different heights. It is weight in kilograms, divided by height in metres squared (Wt (kg)/(Ht (m)$^2$).

**Body image disparagement:** An intense hatred of the size, shape and appearance of parts of the body.

**Body image distortion:** The experience that one's body (or parts of it) is much larger than the numbers (and other people's opinions) suggest.

**Borderline personality disorder:** A condition characterized by impulsive actions, including deliberate self-harm and binge-eating, rapidly shifting moods and chaotic relationships.

*Severe and Enduring Eating Disorder*   Paul Robinson
© 2009 John Wiley & Sons, Ltd

**Buddy:** A person, such as a friend or relative, who is aware of the sufferer's eating disorder and how it is being treated, and provides support.

**Care coordinator:** An individual within a mental health team who takes responsibility for generating and implementing a care plan and arranging regular reviews.

**Care Programme Approach:** A system in some areas of the United Kingdom in which people with severe and enduring mental illness can have their needs met in various domains (qv).

**Carer metaphorical menagerie:** A series of animal metaphors describing how carers act in relation to their eating disordered relatives, including overprotective kangaroos, challenging rhinos, anxious jellyfish, denying ostriches, helpfully nudging dolphins and loyal St Bernards. A suggested addition is the stubborn bulldog.

**CBT:** Cognitive Behaviour Therapy. A psychotherapy based on cognitions, assumptions, beliefs and behaviours, with the aim of influencing negative emotions that relate to inaccurate appraisal of events.

**Chaos and complexity theory:** Mathematical theory used to describe complex systems including weather, economic and social systems, with concepts including sensitive dependence on initial conditions (butterfly effect), strange attractors and fractals.

**Clinical frugality (NL):** The tendency of people with restrictive Anorexia Nervosa to restrict not only food, but all activity seen as extravagance. This may include using heating and transport.

**Coeliac disease:** A condition in which allergy to a constituent of wheat (gluten) leads to failure to absorb nutrition from the intestine.

**Colonic atony:** A condition of the large intestine (colon) in which prolonged abuse of laxatives leads to stretching and poor muscle tone in the colon with resulting constipation and a risk of prolapse (qv) and volvulus (qv).

**Colostomy:** An opening on the skin allowing faeces to empty into a bag sometimes performed when the colon has to be removed.

**Community mental health team:** A team dealing with severe and enduring mental illness, covering a locality with a variety of mental health workers including psychiatrists, psychologists and nurses.

**Co-morbidity:** Conditions from which a patient suffers which are seen as associated with the main condition.

**Condiment abuse:** The excessive use of condiments by people with eating disorders as a response to starvation, and an apparent effort to satisfy the need for taste without consuming calories.

**Cortisol:** A hormone produced by the adrenal gland particularly during physical or psychological stress which can lead to muscle wasting and osteoporosis (qv) in excess.

**Crohn's disease:** An inflammatory disease which can affect any part of the alimentary tract from the mouth to the anus.

**Delayed gastric emptying:** Condition which occurs in Anorexia Nervosa in which food is held in the stomach for longer than usual, causing prolonged feelings of fullness and bloating.

**Delusion:** A false idea, held unshakeably by a person, not shared by that person's social group.

**Diabetes mellitus:** A condition in which insulin either fails to be produced or fails to function normally, leading to abnormally high blood glucose and sometimes disabling complications in bodily systems.

**Dialectical behaviour therapy:** A treatment for borderline personality disorder (qv) comprising weekly individual and group therapy, with emphasis on reducing symptoms and acquiring skills including core mindfulness, emotion regulation, interpersonal effectiveness and distress tolerance.

**Domains:** Areas of life affected by illness and requiring attention by the sufferer, carer and professionals. These include mental and physical health, occupation, accommodation, family and risk assessment.

**DSM IV:** Diagnostic and Statistical Manual of Mental Disorders, version IV. A system of classification of mental disorders, produced by the American Psychiatric Association.

**ECT:** Electric Convulsive Therapy. A treatment involving inducing a modified epileptic fit under anaesthesia, effective in some patients with psychiatric disorder, especially depression.

**Eking behaviour (NL):** The tendency in people with eating disorders, especially Anorexia Nervosa, to stretch out meals so they last as long as possible, reminiscent of behaviour of other starving people with food.

**Electrolytes:** Blood constituents including sodium (qv), potassium (qv), chloride and phosphate (qv) that, when abnormal, can have rapid and dangerous impact on membrane function and impair nerve and heart and kidney function.

**EMDR:** Eye Movement Desensitization and Reprogramming. A method in which techniques of CBT (qv) are combined with visualization and eye movements in the treatment of conditions including PTSD (qv).

**Fractal theory:** Part of chaos and complexity theory (qv) in which the similar patterns at different levels of the structure are studied. Examples are clouds, coastlines, lungs and kidneys.

**Gastro-oesophageal reflux:** Stomach contents rise up into the oesophagus (gullet) causing inflammation and bleeding as a result of weakness of the sphincter (circular muscle) at the junction between the gullet and the stomach.

**Handicap:** The effects of an illness on an individual.

**Handicap, primary:** The effects of the illness itself.

**Handicap, secondary:** The impact of being in the role of a patient for many years.

**Handicap, premorbid:** Pre-existing difficulties such as personality, poverty, poor education.

**Harris–Benedict equation:** An equation that can be used to calculate approximately how many calories an individual would require at rest.

**Hoarding:** The tendency observed in some people with eating disorders to collect food items and keep them, sometimes unopened. Also seen in other forms of starvation. May also apply to money and non-food items.

**Hypoglycaemia:** Low blood sugar (under 4 mmol/l) seen in very underweight patients.

**Hypokalaemia:** Low potassium level (under 3.5 mmol/l) seen as a result of vomiting or laxative abuse. Caused by loss of acid from the stomach or potassium from the bowel.

**Hyponatraemia:** Low sodium level (under 135 mmol/l) seen in patients who waterload (qv). Can lead to epileptic fits.

**ICD 10:** International Classification of Diseases, version 10. The World Health Organization's alternative to the DSM IV (qv).

**Ischaemia:** Lack of adequate blood supply.

**MBT:** Mentalization-Based Therapy. A therapy based on attachment theory used for borderline personality disorder (qv). Mentalization is the capacity, acquired from satisfactory attachment figures, to monitor one's own and others' mental processes.

**Minnesota study:** Classic study performed on conscientious objectors during WWII which showed that many symptoms of eating disorders could be reproduced by starvation.

**NICE:** The National Institute for Health and Clinical Excellence. An organization in the NHS which examines the evidence for and against different treatments and advises on treatment of a range of conditions. www.nice.org.uk.

**Object relations theory:** The idea that the self exists only in relation to other objects, external or internal. Internal objects are internalized external objects, primarily formed from early experiences with parents and other caregivers.

**Oedema:** Swelling due to accumulation of water in parts of the body, usually collecting in the lower parts, such as the ankles, due to gravity.

**Oestrogen:** A female sex hormone, necessary for the normal menstrual cycle.

**Olanzapine:** A drug used in psychosis. Suggested for use in Anorexia Nervosa because of its weight gain side effects and anti-anxiety properties.

**Orthocompulsions (NL):** Extreme tendency to do the right thing, follow established advice, such as exercise more and eat less in the face of evidence that it would be harmful, e.g. by reducing weight.

**Osteomalacia:** Bone disease due to low vitamin D intake in which the protein matrix of bone is not normally filled with calcium salts (rickets in children).

**Osteopaenia:** Moderately increased porousness of bone with increased fracture risk. Seen in post-menopausal women and men and women with Anorexia Nervosa.

**Osteoporosis:** Substantially increased porousness of bone with greatly increased fracture risk. Seen in post-menopausal women and men and women with Anorexia Nervosa.

**Overvalued idea:** Idea which is held to very strongly but which is, at least theoretically, subject to rational argument.

**Paraceptivity (NL):** State in which internal physical signals (such as gastric fullness) are correlated with emotional experiences such as sadness, fatness or anxiety (*para:* beside, *perceive* take cognizance of).

**Phosphate:** An electrolyte (qv) which can fall markedly when a starving person is refed (refeeding syndrome) lead to potential cardiac arrest.

**Potassium:** An electrolyte (qv) mostly within cells, which can fall as a result of vomiting or laxative abuse (see *Hypokalaemia*) causing muscle weakness and spasms, impairment of kidney function, and cardiac changes including cardiac arrest.

**Prolapse:** Condition in which an organ or tissue protrudes into a space it should not occupy (e.g. rectum prolapsing through the anus, womb prolapsing into the vagina).

**Protein losing enteropathy:** Disease of the bowel leading to loss of protein in the faeces. Can be caused by laxative abuse.

**Proton pump inhibitor:** Drug which stops the stomach from producing acid.

**PTSD:** Post-Traumatic Stress Disorder. Range of symptoms including flashbacks of the event, avoidance and phobias and depression which can follow a traumatic event.

**Refeeding syndrome:** Condition occurring during initial refeeding in someone who has had a severely restricted food intake, especially of carbohydrate over a substantial period. Administration of carbohydrate leads to release of insulin and passage of phosphate, potassium and other electrolytes into cells causing potentially fatal hypophosphataemia (low phosphate) and hypokalaemia (low potassium).

**Renin:** Hormone produced by the kidney, an excess of which can cause high blood pressure.

**Schemas:** Mental structures that represent an aspect of the world, including the self. Maladaptive schemas common in people with eating disorders include 'I am a failure', 'I am a bad person'.

**Semi-weightlessness (NL):** The idea that someone spending several years at a low body weight may develop osteoporosis as a result of similar mechanisms to those that cause the condition in weightless astronauts.

**Severe and enduring eating disorder (NL):** An eating disorder that is severe enough to cause significant physical, psychological and social difficulties (see severe and enduring mental illness) and lasts for 10 years or longer. Subtypes include SEED-AN, in which the underlying diagnosis is Anorexia Nervosa, SEED-BN, for those with bulimia nervosa and SEED-BED for those with binge-eating disorder.

**Severe and enduring mental illness:** People with recurrent or severe and enduring mental illness, for example schizophrenia, bipolar affective disorder or organic mental disorder, severe anxiety disorders or severe eating disorders, who have complex needs which may require the continuing care of specialist mental health services working effectively with other agencies.

**Sham feeding:** Animal model in which food is eaten and enters the stomach but is then diverted to a hole in the abdominal wall. The rats will eat almost without end because they are not satiated. Has been suggested as an animal model for bulimia nervosa.

**Sodium:** Electrolyte, mostly outside cells, in the blood. Can fall in patients who drink a lot of water, often to falsify their weight (see Hyponatraemia).

**Somatization disorder:** A somatoform (qv) disorder in which the patient has multiple physical complaints for which numerous doctors are consulted, often not aware of the other consultations. Leads to therapeutic chaos. The complaints may have a medical explanation, but not adequate to explain the severity of the symptom.

**Somatoform disorder:** Set of conditions in which physical symptoms without adequate medical explanation lead to consultation. These include somatization disorder (qv), conversion disorder (e.g. paralysis with no medical cause), hypochondriasis, body dysmorphic disorder (distorted view of a part of the body) and pain disorder.

**Spironolactone:** Diuretic drug that works by blocking the effect of aldosterone (qv).

**Stigma:** Severe social disapproval, criticism and rejection of persons with mental illness.

**Strange attractors:** Mathematical constructs that reflect behaviour of chaotic systems (see chaos and complexity theory).

**SUED (NL):** Severe and Unstable Eating Disorder. Patients with eating disorders that require constant or frequent inpatient care with high levels of supervision to prevent harm.

**SUSS test (NL):** Stand Up Squat Stand test to monitor muscle power in patients with Anorexia Nervosa, especially < BMI 14. See text for description and rating scale.

**TMJ syndrome:** Temporomandibular Joint Syndrome. Pain in the joint linking the jaw to the skull, which can occur due to frequent and prolonged chewing and spitting of food.

**Vitamin D:** A fat-soluble vitamin essential for calcium absorption and bone health.

**Volvulus:** Twisting of the colon as a result of laxative abuse (see *colonic atony* and *prolapse*).

**Waterloading:** Practice of drinking large amounts of water in order to falsify weight. Maximum recorded 9.5 l.

# References

Abraham, S. F., Brown, T., Boyd, C. *et al.* (2006) Quality of life: eating disorders. *Australia and New Zealand Journal of Psychiatry*, **40**, 150–55.

Affenito, S. G., Dohm, F. A., Crawford, P. B. *et al.* (2002) Macronutrient intake in Anorexia Nervosa: The National Heart, Lung, and Blood Institute Growth and Health Study. *Journal of Pediatrics*, **141**, 701–5.

American Psychiatric Association (1994) *The Diagnostic and Statistical Manual of Mental Disorders*, 4th edn, American Psychiatric Press.

Asen, E. and Schmidt, U. (2005) Special issue: multi-family therapy in Anorexia Nervosa. *Journal of Family Therapy*, **27** (2), 101–3.

Barr, W. (2001) Physical health of people with severe mental illness (letter). *BMJ: British Medical Association*, **323**, 231.

Bateman, A. and Fonagy, P. (2004) *Psychotherapy for Borderline Personality Disorder: Mentalization Based Treatment*, Oxford University Press.

Beck, A., Steer, R. and Brown, G. (1996) *Manual for Beck Depression Inventory-II*, Psychological Corporation, San Antonio.

Birmingham, C. L., Su, J., Hlynsky, J. A. *et al.* (2005) The mortality rate from Anorexia Nervosa. *International Journal of Eating Disorders*, **38**, 143–46.

Bo-Linn, G. W., Santa Ana, C. A., Morawski, S. G. and Fordtran, J. S. (1983) Purging and calorie absorption in bulimic patients and normal women. *Annals of Internal Medicine*, **99**, 14–17.

Bratman, S. and Knight, D. (2001) *Health Food Junkies: Orthorexia Nervosa: Overcoming the Obsession with Healthful Eating*, Broadway Books, New York.

Claudino, A. M., Hay, P., Lima, M. S. *et al.* (2006) Antidepressants for Anorexia Nervosa. *Cochrane Database of Systematic Reviews* [Online], no. 1, p. CD004365, 129 refs, IS.

Colahan, M. and Robinson, P. (2002). Multi-family groups in the treatment of young adults with eating disorders. *Journal of Family Therapy*, **24**, 17–30

*Severe and Enduring Eating Disorder*    Paul Robinson
© 2009 John Wiley & Sons, Ltd

Crisp, A. H. (2000) Changing minds: every family in the land - an update on the college campaign. *Psychiatric Bulletin*, **24**, 267–68.

Crisp, A. H., Callender, J. S., Halek, C. and Hsu, L. K. (1992) Long-term mortality in Anorexia Nervosa. A 20-year follow-up of the St George's and Aberdeen cohorts. *The British Journal of Psychiatry*, **161**, 104–7.

Currin, L., Schmidt, U., Treasure, J. and Jick, H. (2005) Time trends in eating disorders incidence. *The British Journal of Psychiatry*, **186**, 132–35.

Dare, C. and Eisler, I. (2000) A multi-family group day treatment programme for adolescent eating disorder. *European Eating Disorders Review*, **8**, 4–18.

de la Rie, S., Noordenbos, G., Donker, M. and van Furth, E. (2006) The patient's view on quality of life and eating disorders. *International Journal of Eating Disorders*, **40**, 13–20.

Department of Health (1990) *NHS and Community Care Act*, HMSO, London.

Department of Health (1999a) National service framework for mental health: modern standards and service models. HSC 1999/223.

Department of Health (1999b) *Effective Care Co-ordination in Mental Health Services: Modernising the Care Programme Approach*, DoH, London.

Elvevåg, B. and Goldberg, T. E. (2000) Cognitive impairment in schizophrenia is the core of the disorder. *Critical Reviews in Neurobiology*, **14**, 1–21.

Fonagy, P. and Target, M. (2003) *Psychoanalytic Theories: Perspectives from Developmental Pyschopathology (Whurr Series in Psychoanalysis)*, Routledge.

Galusca, B., Zouch, M., Germain, N. *et al.* (2008) Constitutional thinness: unusual human phenotype of low bone quality. *The Journal of Clinical Endocrinology and Metabolism*, **93**, 110–17.

Garner, D. M., Olmsted, M. P. and Polivy, J. (1983) Development and validation of a multidimensional eating disorder inventory for Anorexia Nervosa and bulimia. *International Journal of Eating Disorders*, **2**, 15–34.

Gottlieb, S. (2001) Oestrogen replacement increases cancer risk, study shows. *BMJ: British Medical Association*, **322**, 756.

Hall, S. (2000) Scandal of Britain's ballet schools: 15-year study says young dancers are pressured to become anorexic. *The Guardian*, Thursday, 29 June.

Harris, R. B. (1990) Role of set-point theory in regulation of body weight. *FASEB Journal*, **4**, 3310–8.

Hearing, S. D. (2004) Refeeding syndrome. *BMJ: British Medical Association*, **328**, 908–9.

Heizer, W. D., Warshaw, A. L., Waldmann, R. A. *et al.* (1968) Protein-losing gastroenteropathy and malabsorption associated with factitious diarrhea. *Annals of Internal Medicine*, **68**, 839–52.

Henderson, M. and Freeman, C. P. (1987) A self-rating scale for bulimia. The 'BITE'. *The British Journal of Psychiatry*, **150**, 18–24.

Hirsch, S. R. (1976) The care of schizophrenic patients outside of the hospital: Research results and basic principles. *Nervenarzt*, **47** (8), 469–76.

Hodes, M., Timimi, S. and Robinson, P. H. (1997) Children of mothers with eating disorders: a preliminary study. *European Eating Disorders Review*, 5, 11–24.

Hodgson, R. and Rachman, S. (1977) Obsessional compulsive complaints. *Behaviour Research and Therapy*, 15, 389–95.

Holloway, F. (2005) The Forgotten Need for Rehabilitation in Contemporary Mental Health Services. A position statement from the Executive Committee of the Faculty of Rehabilitation and Social Psychiatry, Royal College of Psychiatrists.

Hsu, L. K. G., Kaye, W. and Weltzin, T. (1993) Are the eating disorders related to obsessive compulsive disorder? *International Journal of Eating Disorders*, 14, 305–18.

Keilen, M., Treasure, T., Schmidt, U. and Treasure, J. (1994) Quality of life measurements in eating disorders, angina, and transplant candidates: are they comparable? *Journal of Royal Society of Medicine*, 87 (8), 441–44.

Keller, T. S., Strauss A. M., Szpalski, M. (1992) Prevention of bone loss and muscle atrophy during manned space flight. *Microgravity Q.*, 2, 89–102.

Keys, A., Brozel, J., Henschel, A. *et al.* (1950) *The Biology of Human Starvation*, University of Minnesota Press.

Kouba, S., Hallstrom, T., Lindholm, C. and Hirschberg, A. L. (2005) Pregnancy and neonatal outcomes in women with eating disorders. *Obstetrics and Gynecology*, 105, 255–60.

Lacey, J. H. and Evans, C. (1986) The impulsivist: a multi-impulsive personality disorder. *British Journal of Addiction*, 81, 641–9.

Lacey, J. H. and Read, T. (1993) Multi-impulsive bulimia: description of an inpatient eclectic treatment programme and a pilot follow-up study of its efficacy. *Eating Disorders Review*, 1 (1), 22–31.

Lacey, J. H. and Smith, G. (1987) Bulimia nervosa. The impact of pregnancy on mother and baby. *The British Journal of Psychiatry*, 150, 777–81.

Lewis, G. and Appleby, L. (1988) Personality disorder: the patients psychiatrists dislike. *The British Journal of Psychiatry*, 153, 44–49.

Linehan, M. (1993) *Cognitive Behavioural Treatment of Borderline Personality Disorder (Diagnosis & Treatment of Mental Disorders)*, Guilford.

McMahon, B. (2006) Catwalk ban on the skinny model in Italy. *The Observer*, Sunday, 3 December.

Milosevic, A. (1999) Eating disorders and the dentist. *British Dental Journal*, 186, 109–13.

Minuchin, S. (1990) *Psychosomatic Families: Anorexia Nervosa in Context*, Harvard University Press.

Mond, J., Owen, C., Hay, P. *et al.* (2005) Assessing quality of life in eating disorders patients. *Quality of Life Research*, 14 (1), 171–78.

Morgan, J. F., Lacey, J. H. and Chung, E. (2006) Risk of postnatal depression, miscarriage, and preterm birth in bulimia nervosa: retrospective controlled study. *Psychosomatic Medicine*, 68, 487–92.

National Audit Office (2005) A Safer Place for Patients: Learning to Improve Patient Safety. Report by the Comptroller and Auditor General, HC 456 2005-2006, 3 November.

National Collaborating Centre for Mental Health (2004) Eating Disorders: Core interventions in the treatment and management of Anorexia Nervosa, bulimia nervosa and related eating disorders. National Clinical Practice Guideline Number CG9, The British Psychological Society & The Royal College of Psychiatrists.

National Collaborating Centre for Mental Health (2005) Post-traumatic stress disorder (PTSD). The management of PTSD in adults and children in primary and secondary care Clinical Guideline 26.

Parker, G., Rosen, A., Emdur, N. and Hadzi-Pavlovic, D. (1991) The Life Skills Profile: psychometric properties of a measure assessing function and disability in schizophrenia. *Acta Psychiatrica Scandinavica*, **83**, 145–52.

Payne-James, J. J., Grimble, G. K., Forbes, A. and Silk, D. B. A. (2008) *Artificial Nutrition Support in Clinical Practice*, 3rd edn, Cambridge University Press.

Petot, J.-M. and Trollope, C. (1991) *Melanie Klein: The Ego and the Good Object 1932-1960*, Vol. **2**, International Universities Press.

Powell, J. T. and Greenhalgh, R. M. (1994) Arterial bypass surgery and smokers. *BMJ: British Medical Association*, **308**, 607–8.

Ratnasuriya, R. H., Eisler, I., Szmukler, G. I. and Russell, G. F. M. (1991) Anorexia Nervosa: outcome and prognostic factors after 20 years. *The British Journal of Psychiatry*, **158**, 495–502.

Robertson, R. and Combs, A. (1995) *Chaos Theory in Psychology and the Life Sciences*, Laurence Erlbaum Associates, Hove.

Robinson, P. H. (1989) Perceptivity and paraceptivity during measurement of gastric emptying in anorexia and bulimia nervosa. *British Journal of Psychiatry*, **154**, 400–405.

Robinson, P. H. (2006a) *Community Treatment of Eating Disorders*, John Wiley & Sons, Ltd, Chichester.

Robinson, P. H. (2006b) *Community Treatment of Eating Disorders. Severe and Enduring Eating Disorders*, John Wiley & Sons, Ltd, Chichester, pp. 165–76.

Robinson, P. H., Barrett, J. and Clarke, M. (1988) Determinants of delayed gastric emptying in Anorexia Nervosa and bulimia nervosa. *Gut*, **29**, 458–64.

Rosen, A., Hadzi-Pavlovic, D. and Parker, G. (1989) The life skills profile: a measure assessing function and disability in schizophrenia. *Schizophrenia Bulletin*, **15** (2), 325–37.

Russell, G. F., Szmukler, G. I., Dare, C. and Eisler, I. (1987) An evaluation of family therapy in Anorexia Nervosa and bulimia nervosa. *Archives of General Psychiatry*, **44** (12), 1047–56.

Serpell, L. and Treasure, J. (2002) Bulimia Nervosa: friend or foe? The pros and cons of Bulimia Nervosa. *International Journal of Eating Disorders*, **32**, 164–70.

Serpell, L., Treasure, J., Teasdale, J. and Sullivan, V. (1999) Anorexia Nervosa: friend or foe. *International Journal of Eating Disorders*, **25**, 177–86.

Shetty, P. S. and James W. P. T. (1994) Food and Agriculture Organization of the United Nations, Body mass index – A measure of chronic energy deficiency in adults FAO Food and Nutrition paper 56, 1994, Chapter 7 BMI distribution in developed and developing countries. http://www.fao.org/docrep/t1970e/t1970e08.htm (accessed 4 October 2008).

Skevington, S. M. (1999) Measuring quality of life in Britain: an introduction to the WHOQOL-100. *Journal of Psychosomatic Research*, **47** (5), 449–59.

Skevington, S. M. and Wright, A. (2001) Changes in the quality of life of patients receiving anti-depressant medication in primary care: validating the WHOQOL-100. *British Journal of Psychiatry*, **178**, 261–26.

Solomon, C. G. (2002) Bisphosphonates and osteoporosis. *New England Journal of Medicine*, **346**, 642.

Stein, A., Woolley, H., Murray, L. *et al.* (2001) Influence of psychiatric disorder on the controlling behaviour of mothers with 1-year-old infants. A study of women with maternal eating disorder, postnatal depression and a healthy comparison group. *British Journal of Psychiatry*, **179**, 157–62.

Steinhausen, H. C. (2002) The outcome of Anorexia Nervosa in the 20th century. *American Journal of Psychiatry*, **159** (8), 1284–93.

Stevenson, J. C. (2005) Justification for the use of HRT in the long-term prevention of osteoporosis. *Maturitas*, **51**, 113–26.

Sullivan, P. F., Bulik, C. M., Fear, J. L. and Pickering, A. (1998) Outcome of Anorexia Nervosa: a case-control study. *American Journal of Psychiatry*, **155**, 939–46.

Theander, S. (1985) Outcome and prognosis in anorexia and bulimia: some results of previous investigations, compared with those of a Swedish long-term study. *Journal of Psychiatric Research*, **9**, 493–508.

Thornton, C. and Russell, J. (1997) Obsessive compulsive comorbidity in the dieting disorders. *International Journal of Eating Disorders*, **21**, 83–87.

Thornton, J. F., Seeman, M. V. and Plummer, E. D. (2007) *Schizophrenia: Rehabilitation*. Merrell Dow Pharmaceuticals ( Canada).

Treasure, J., Schmidt, U. and Hugo, P. (2005) Mind the gap: service transition and interface problems for patients with eating disorders. *The British Journal of Psychiatry*, **187**, 398–400.

Ward, A., Ramsay, R., Turnbull, S. *et al.* (2001) Attachment in Anorexia Nervosa: A transgenerational perspective. *British Journal of Medical Psychology*, **74**, 497–505.

Whelan, E. and Cooper, P. J. (2000) The association between childhood feeding problems and maternal eating disorder: a community study. *Psychological Medicine*, **30**, 69–77.

Wise, J. (2001) UK government and doctors agree to end "blame culture". *BMJ: British Medical Association*, **323**, 9.

World Health Organization (1992) ICD-10: The ICD-10 Classification of Mental and Behavioural Disorders: Clinical Descriptions and Diagnostic Guidelines (Paperback), World Health Organization.

Yager, J. (2007) Management of patients with chronic, intractable eating disorders, in *Clinical Manual of Eating Disorders* (eds J. Yager and P. S. Powers), American Psychiatric Publishing, London.

Young, N., Formica, C., Szmukler, G. and Seeman, E. (1994) Bone density at weight-bearing and nonweight-bearing sites in ballet dancers: the effects of exercise, hypogonadism, and body weight. *The Journal of Clinical Endocrinology and Metabolism*, **78**, 449–54.

Young, R. C., Gibbs, J., Antin, J. *et al.* (1974) Absence of satiety during sham feeding in the rat. *Journal of Comparative and Physiological Psychology*, **87** (5), 795–800.

Zehnacker, C. and Bemis-Dougherty, A. (2007) Effect of weighted exercises on bone mineral density in post menopausal women: a systematic review. *Journal of Geriatric Physical Therapy*, **30**, 79–88.

# Index

*Severe and Enduring Eating Disorder*   Paul Robinson
© 2009 John Wiley & Sons, Ltd